STATEMENT CONCERNING PUBLICATIONS OF RUSSELL SAGE FOUNDATION

Russell Sage Foundation was established in 1907 by Mrs. Russell Sage "for the improvement of social and living conditions in the United States of America." In carrying out its purpose the Foundation maintains a staff which, among other duties, conducts studies of social conditions, authorized by the General Director, where new information, its analysis and interpretation seem necessary in order to formulate and advance practicable measures aimed at improvement. From time to time the Foundation publishes the results of these studies in book or pamphlet form.

In formulating the problem for study, in mapping out a plan of work on it, in collecting facts, in drawing conclusions, and in the presentation of findings, authors of Foundation studies, who are always either members of the staff or specially commissioned research workers, have the benefit of the criticism and advice of their colleagues in the organization. Full freedom is given research workers for the final decision on all of these steps, and in presenting and interpreting both factual material and conclusions in their own way. While the general responsibility for management of the Foundation is vested in the Board of Trustees, the responsibility for facts, conclusions, and interpretations rests with the research workers alone and not upon the Foundation, its trustees, or other members of the staff. Publication under the imprint of the Foundation does not imply agreement by the organization or its members with opinions or interpretations of authors. It does imply that care has been taken that the research on which a book is based has been thoroughly done.

STUDIES IN PUBLIC RELATIONS

Prepared by the Department of Social Work
Interpretation, Mary Swain Routzahn, Director

A STUDY IN PUBLIC RELATIONS
  By Harold P. Levy

  Case History of the Relations Maintained Between a
  Department of Public Assistance and the People of a
  State

BUILDING A POPULAR MOVEMENT
  By Harold P. Levy

  The Public Relations of the Boy Scouts of America

TOWARD PUBLIC UNDERSTANDING OF CASEWORK
  By Viola Paradise

  A Study of Casework Interpretation in Cleveland

Published by

RUSSELL   SAGE   FOUNDATION

TOWARD PUBLIC UNDERSTANDING OF CASEWORK

A Study of Casework Interpretation in Cleveland

By

Viola Paradise, Research Associate
Department of Social Work Interpretation
Russell Sage Foundation

New York

RUSSELL SAGE FOUNDATION

1948

WM. F.FELL CO., PRINTERS
PHILADELPHIA

CONTENTS

3

92430

CONTENTS

CONTENTS

5

CONTENTS

ADVISORY COMMITTEE

CHAIRMAN: Mrs. Everett Rhodes Castle, chairman, Volunteer Advisory Committee, Central Volunteer Bureau, Welfare Federation of Cleveland; formerly staff member, Family Service Association of Cleveland

SECRETARY: Anna B. Beattie, educational secretary, Family Service Association of Cleveland

EX OFFICIO MEMBER: Rev. Howard M. Wells, D.D., formerly chairman, Casework Council, Welfare Federation of Cleveland; chairman, Interpretation Committee, Welfare Federation of Cleveland

MEMBERS:

Mrs. Laura Parmenter Andrews, formerly director, Community Relations, Children's Services of Cleveland

Mrs. Lucia J. Bing, secretary, Committees on the Aged and Chronically Ill, Welfare Federation of Cleveland

Raymond A. Bruner, publicity director, Western Reserve University

Jack Yeaman Bryan, formerly public relations director, Welfare Federation of Cleveland

Mrs. John B. Dempsey, board member, Family Service Association of America; board member, Family Service Association of Cleveland

Daniel R. Elliott, secretary, Casework and Children's Councils, Welfare Federation of Cleveland; formerly assistant executive director, Children's Services of Cleveland

7

James E. Ewers, director and superintendent, Cuyahoga County Child Welfare Board

Belle Greve, executive secretary, Cleveland Rehabilitation Center

Dorothy Kimmel, Aid for Dependent Children, administered by Juvenile Court

Mrs. Helen Allyn MacDonald, columnist, Cleveland Press

Mary I. Madsen, case consultant, Social Service Department, University Hospitals of Cleveland

Florence M. Mason, assistant director, Catholic Charities Bureau of Cleveland

Regis McAuley, Cleveland News

W. Thomas McCullough, research secretary, Welfare Federation of Cleveland

Janelle Moser, formerly assistant, Publicity Department, Cleveland Community Fund

Mrs. Mildred Midnight Ross, director, Personal Service, and case consultant, Young Women's Christian Association of Cleveland

Todd Simon, reporter and special writer, Cleveland Plain Dealer

Cornelius Utz, formerly assistant director, Cleveland Youth Bureau

Mrs. Rae Carp Weil, general director, Jewish Family Service Association of Cleveland

Henry L. Zucker, associate director, Jewish Welfare Federation of Cleveland; formerly secretary, Casework and Children's Councils, Welfare Federation of Cleveland

8

INTRODUCTION

THIS book addresses itself primarily to those who wish to bring about a wider public knowledge of social casework. To achieve this understanding is a concern of the profession of social work. It is also the problem of those who sponsor casework agencies, and of all who as staff members or volunteers represent these agencies in contacts with the public.

Although the book is directed especially to the casework field, its analysis of how casework is interpreted in one community has importance for all branches of social work.

In this study more consideration is given to content than is usually found in texts on public information. About twenty years ago the Department of Surveys and Exhibits, the forerunner of the Department of Social Work Interpretation, which sponsors this volume, published a comprehensive book on publicity methods.[1] Its function as stated in the Preface was "to discuss the technique of imparting information about social facts and ideas already gathered and appraised."

The limitation of the discussion of publicity to its presentation, omitting any consideration of content, takes for granted that social agencies when they wish to go before the public have their facts well in hand and lack only the skill and the "know-how" of getting

[1] Routzahn, Mary Swain and Routzahn, Evart G., Publicity for Social Work. Russell Sage Foundation, New York, 1928.

9

information to the people for whom it is intended in an interesting and understandable form.

The Department's experience in the twenty-year period since its book on methods was published has revealed that suitable facts are seldom easily accessible when needed for publicity. This is especially true of social casework. Here, figures which do not seem to be needed by casework practitioners, but are important in making reports of need and of accomplishment convincing to the public, must be especially gathered and appraised for publicity purposes. Public agencies are, on the whole, better equipped than private agencies in this regard. But even the statistical reports of welfare departments, prepared because they are required by law, do not always tell the public what it should know.

The interpreter may not take for granted that even the goals of a social agency have been carefully formulated or that the problems it deals with, and the kinds of people it serves, are a matter of record. For the growth and change in modern social work has been so rapid that not only is social work ahead of its public; it is often ahead of its own recording of social work experience and philosophy.

Publicity about social work appears most often as a part of a money-raising campaign. Drive psychology simplifies the content of an appeal as much as possible. The story to be told on these occasions seems obvious, requiring only selection of a few instances of need and service to support requests for funds. As new relations with the public bring new kinds of questions, and as many new groups become associated with social work as co-operators, clients, and sponsors, the content of public information needs to be more specific, better documented, and more varied.

This volume regards content and method of presentation as inseparable, but it places its chief emphasis on the content of casework interpretation. It considers these elements in relation to the existing public opinion and knowledge of casework in the community studied, and to the kind of public relations casework agencies wish to establish.

Cleveland was chosen for our purpose of examining the public relations of one form of social service because conditions for study were excellent there. Cleveland social workers wished to take part in our venture. Cleveland's standards of casework are high. Its social agencies, of all denominations, public and private, work well together; and a strong Welfare Federation—one of the earliest to be established— gives impetus and direction to their co-operation.

This habit of co-operation in the social work field is characteristic of the city as a whole. Cleveland's many civic and cultural institutions too—such as the libraries, the Playhouse (Cleveland's civic theater), the press, the radio—lend themselves as a matter of course to social work projects. Although the population of Greater Cleveland in 1946 passed the million mark, it has still kept much of the neighborliness of the small town. Its pioneering civic spirit and tradition of service are outstanding, and have been since the turn of the century, when a group of civic-minded men of affairs began to channel the city's natural neighborliness toward effective action. This group included Cleveland's famous reform mayor, Tom L. Johnson, and Newton D. Baker, and in the social work field James F. Jackson, who, with his vivid personality and combination of imagination, common sense, and courage, laid the groundwork for many accomplishments of later years.

Our study of the public relations of casework, coming at a time when Cleveland was pushing forward its casework frontiers, found ready co-operation in the Welfare Federation, in the individual casework agencies, and in the community in general. The Federation's well-organized Interpretation Committee appointed for our study a special Advisory Committee selected from its administrative staff, its casework and children's councils, and also representatives of Cleveland's three newspapers, and several public relations specialists.

This was an active, working committee. Besides its advisory function, it provided much background material: a review of casework developments in Cleveland in the past fifteen years; an account of social and economic conditions affecting casework; material on the development of casework projects in certain areas of the city; on the use of casework in schools, in children's institutions, in hospitals, and other organizations.

The Committee also took part in several special projects and experiments. On one, through a subcommittee of caseworkers from different fields, it worked out a descriptive statement about casework as it is done today. Later, a writers' subcommittee made up of representatives of Cleveland's three newspapers and two public relations specialists joined these caseworkers and revised and rewrote the statement for popular uses.

Another experiment had to do with the effectiveness of interpretation by conversations, and was
undertaken by the caseworkers in three agencies—
the Family Service Association of Cleveland, the
Jewish Family Service Association, and the Cuyahoga
County Relief Bureau. In the two private family
agencies, the clerical staff also participated.

Another project—carried out by a member of the
Committee working with a school principal and a
psychologist of a Cleveland agency—was concerned
with the attitudes of children toward social work.

A project which came out of our study but was
carried on independently grew from a suggestion of
the Plain Dealer's representative on the Advisory
Committee: to devise a poll of opinion, testing what
the public knew and felt about casework. This idea
developed into a poll of opinions about a wide range
of health and welfare subjects, but was limited to the
women of Cleveland. Several of its queries brought
material of value to our study.

This book is the third to be published of a group
of studies in public relations, each dealing with
a different aspect of social work, each treating
the subject on a different geographical level. The
first, A Study in Public Relations, by Harold P. Levy,
dealt with public relations in a state department of
public assistance; the second, Building a Popular
Movement, also written by Mr. Levy, with a national movement in the group-work field; and the
present volume by Viola Paradise, with a specific
kind of service carried on by both public and private
agencies in one community.

It is our hope that not only persons working in the special field with which each study is concerned, but also students and practitioners of community organization, social work administration, and public relations, will find these studies useful. They invite and assist persons working in these areas to explore the function of public relations in specific agencies and in social work as a whole. Social organizations desiring to deal more adequately with their public relations problems are frequently uncertain as to what are desirable qualifications of workers to whom public relations planning and practice may be intrusted; how much to expect of a public relations program in carrying forward the agency objectives; and how the public relations assignment fits into the agency's administrative pattern.

These studies are only a beginning of the kind of research needed to find answers to such questions. Perhaps their publication will stimulate other studies out of which public relations practice will achieve a much greater usefulness and stability than it now has.

We wish to express our thanks to the members of our Cleveland Advisory Committee whose help is noted frequently in the pages of this book. Individually, and as a group, they collected information, carried on experiments, and in many other ways forwarded our study. We wish, especially, to thank Anna B. Beattie, who as secretary to the Committee worked closely with us throughout the project.

Many persons not on the Committee gave valuable help. We wish to thank the staff of the Welfare Federation; Helen W. Hanchette, executive secretary, Family Service Association of Cleveland, and several of her staff; the staff members of other Cleveland agencies, especially the Jewish Family Service Association and the Cuyahoga County Relief Bureau.

We are also very appreciative of the help of Mrs. Sallie Bright, executive director, National Publicity Council for Health and Welfare Services; Mrs. Henrietta L. Gordon, information and publications secretary, Child Welfare League of America; Florence Hollis, formerly director of publications, Family Service Association of America; Marion Voges, formerly public relations consultant, Family Service Association of America; Frances Taussig, executive director, Jewish Family Service, Inc., of New York City; and many others who contributed information, time, and wisdom to our study.

Mary Swain Routzahn, *Director*
Department of Social Work Interpretation

CHAPTER I

AN OLD TRADITION AND A
NEW PHILOSOPHY

CASEWORK, the most widely practiced form of social work, is the least understood. This is true even though, during the past half-dozen years, it has begun to venture beyond its home grounds in family and children's service agencies, and to find a foothold in schools, institutions, group-work agencies, industries, unions, the armed services, veterans' service agencies, and other outposts which the social worker of the 1920's could hardly have envisaged. It has emerged from its matrix of charity into a service in itself. Now it must be understood for itself: a method of helping people in many kinds of need to find their own way toward the goal of meeting those needs; a service not confined to one kind of social agency, but applicable in countless situations, and under many new auspices.

To examine and report upon the ways in which social caseworkers and social casework agencies go about the task of securing public understanding, and the ways in which the usefulness of casework has grown through good understanding, is the purpose of this book. It draws its material primarily from Cleveland, but it is written against a background of general study of casework and its interpretation.

LOOKING BACKWARD

The economic ups and downs and emotional turbulence of America's recent history—whether in depression or in times of high wartime earnings, or in the confusions of the postwar years—all created new needs for casework, and forced upon it a new pace of development and new requirements for public understanding.

Casework's slow, uneven growth began in social agencies whose chief purpose was to relieve material distress. Whenever these agencies took their story to the public, it was to get funds to relieve such distress. All down the years people supported them out of pity for the hungry, the cold, the orphaned, the abused, the erring. But the public learned little or nothing of casework itself; for until the depression it was deeply buried under the relief-giving function of the private family agencies, and nearly nonexistent in the predepression public poor-relief facilities.

Caseworkers, however, in their ministering to material needs, whether of poverty-stricken families or dependent or neglected children, long ago became aware that many human problems, though emphasized by poverty, existed irrespective of poverty. Under similar economic pressures one family, one person, would go under, and others would somehow manage to get along. The same physical environmental forces which precipitated some into dependency and into various despairs, left others with the capacity to struggle through. The caseworkers learned —without in any way minimizing economic and other outer forces—that forces inside the personality, too,

17

and the impact of personality upon personality inside the family caused the helplessness or the deterioration of some and not of others. They began to study these forces.

They re-explored their basic philosophy which had grown, in part, out of studies of social conditions which so profoundly affected the families they helped. In the 1920's they began to draw upon the new discoveries of psychiatry. Social change, though imperative and constantly to be worked for, was not enough. Caseworkers, examining their failures and their successes, now felt impelled to a new research. It was as if they said, "Let us re-examine human nature. Let us see what people really are like, and on the basis of these realities, discover sturdier ways of helping them."

But though in committees, in conferences, in schools of social work, they were developing these new ways, they were not ready to talk about them except in inner professional circles, and to the boards which had to finance their experiments. Their progress was, perforce, slow and groping; and perhaps in its early stages it needed to be sheltered from public scrutiny.

Meanwhile material needs continued to out-clamor the less obvious though no less basic personality needs. And until the depression of the thirties forced the development of public assistance programs, people thought of the private family agency, by whatever name, as a dispenser of relief, as the distributor and protector of the funds contributed to lighten the miseries of poverty. They thought of the child-care agency as a provider of food and shelter, usually in an institution.

18

When the community chests came into being,[1] the agencies were content to let them play up the physical needs of their clients, as the agencies themselves had done. For the great bulk of the money they then spent went to provide for physical needs.

No wonder that the chest campaigns helped to entrench the idea that the family agency existed only to relieve desperate want. No wonder that the money-raisers reached for the most agile purse-opening symbol they could find—usually a pitiable child with outstretched hand. The appeal worked. It still works so well that some chests hesitate to replace it with the far better story casework now can tell.

In the beginning this appeal had a basic integrity. But as the chief emphasis of the private family agencies shifted from relief to help with problems of personal or family adjustment, and the emphasis of the child-care agencies shifted from custodial care for children to a service to help parents find the best way in which their children's needs could be met, the old appeal lost what virtue it had had, and served only to maintain a mistaken attitude in the public mind. This attitude persists even today, despite the spreading range of casework service, and its widening support.

But new attitudes are beginning to gain strength. More and more people are learning that casework has ceased to be an appendage to a charity provided out of pity or benevolence by the well-to-do for the deserving poor; that in private agencies, it is a service supported by an ever-growing number of community chest contributors from nearly every economic level,

[1] This method of fund-raising originated in Cleveland in 1919.

19

and that it aims to be available to anyone with personal troubles irrespective of economic need; that in those public assistance agencies where casework accompanies relief—still too few—it is tax-supported by everybody, and is available as a right to anybody in need.

The Depression Forces a New Approach

The depression of the thirties, which plunged one-sixth of our population into dependency, made it clear that private philanthropy could not begin to cope with the survival needs of its victims. It placed the responsibility for relief upon the public conscience and the public purse.

The taking over by government of responsibility for material need freed the private family service agencies not only of a great financial burden but also of the mass of detail in the mechanics of relief-giving. It allowed them to give much fuller thought to the personality needs of their clients, and to develop the more constructive aspects of casework, whether or not financial help was involved.

It also forced them to reach out for better and wider public understanding. If the private family agencies were to hold their ground, if they were to improve and extend their ways of helping people, they must let people know what they did, and why. Clients who needed casework services must know where to find them. Contributors must be shown the value of these services. And, unless such wisdom as the agencies had accumulated through the years were to be jettisoned, they must build up in the public mind a continuing confidence in their judgment and experience.

Nearly all the private family agencies did manage to survive the amputation of relief as their major function. They survived, however, not because of any wide public recognition of the need for casework, or knowledge about it, but because they had proved their worth in the past, and because their communities or their supporting community chests were willing to take their word about the need for services other than relief.

Many private family service agencies had achieved a high degree of public confidence and these contributed much to the newly established public assistance agencies. They provided executives and a nucleus of trained staff. In some communities the whole private agency was assigned to administer public relief, and subsidized by government for that purpose.

PENALTIES FOR SILENCE

Even the best family agencies had, however, failed to establish themselves in the public mind and in the minds of legislators as expert in their field, and for this failure millions of relief clients paid dearly. Because of it public relief in many communities, sometimes in whole states, recapitulated the blunders which private philanthropy made on its groping way up from the basket days of its Ladies-Bountiful to its current—though by no means final—competence. Relief in kind, instead of cash; relief in humiliating driblets, instead of relief based upon intelligently worked-out budgets; relief dispensed by persons utterly inexperienced in helping those in distress—

these are some of the miseries which depression victims might have been spared if, through the years, the private agencies had built up strong groups of well-informed supporters. Such groups, ready to goad the public conscience and to guide it along a well-charted course, would have carried weight with legislators and administrators of the new publicly supported relief agencies.

The caseworkers, too, who went into the public field, suddenly face to face with doubting politicians, jealous untrained fellow workers, and county and state boards who did not understand their language, would have found their new tasks easier. As it was, they had not the time, the experience, or the required skills to tell grudging skeptics just how casework knowledge applied to public relief would save not only the self-respect of recipients, but also prevent much expensive and muddling confusion in administering relief.

Not only public assistance but private family and child-care agencies and other agencies and institutions in which casework is practiced have been hobbled by lack of public understanding. Confronted with the need to secure such understanding, they have encountered difficulties. Information and publicity in the ordinary sense do not suffice. You cannot just tell people about casework. You have to *interpret* it. For casework, a subtle service, not to groups but to individuals, gives something particular to each person it helps. Its uses grow with the experience and skills of its practitioners, for it is a developing, not a static way of helping people. And it is based upon changing concepts of how to help them, and upon a growing

22

knowledge of human nature. Casework is nothing to "come and see." It has nothing to *show*—no groups of people having fun, no equipment, no gadgets. It is not photogenic.

Nor is it a service which, without interpretation, people easily relate to their own needs. On the contrary, they tend to regard it as something for special classes of people whom they now designate by the condescending word "underprivileged." Many still look upon the caseworker as a person hired to investigate the "worthiness" of applicants; to help those who have fallen into need "through no fault of their own" with money and advice about spending it, and advice about the conduct of their lives.

But caseworkers have traveled a long way ahead of the public's image of them. They are not—as were the charity workers of earlier days—concerned with "worthiness." Rather, "they search for *worth* in people as something to work with, not worthiness as a basis for selecting people to be helped."[1] Nor, to them, does it matter whose fault brings a client to their doors. And—in most branches of casework—they have discarded authoritative advice, having learned that the effective way of helping people is to enable them to discover and use their own strength to help themselves.

When government took over the responsibility for relief, the family casework agencies, absorbed in techniques, in learning better how to help their clients, were for the most part ill equipped for the suddenly urgent need to secure public understanding.

[1] Routzahn, Mary Swain, "Publicizing Human Needs," in *Public Opinion Quarterly*, October, 1937.

The depression challenge "What is there for you to do, now that the public agency provides relief?" put them on the defensive.

Trying to answer it, some of them floundered about, claiming in a sort of panic that they did their work better than the public agency, stressing the superiority of their trained caseworkers over the hordes of untrained relief investigators. Some agencies, in their appeal for continuing support, gave disproportionate emphasis to services they maintained as supplements to the main body of casework—for instance, vocational guidance, homemaker services, budgeting and nutrition counseling, or nursing.

Wiser agencies realized that they must re-examine their experience and learn to select from it information which would show the public the validity and usefulness of casework.

Here they met new obstacles. For one thing, they had only just begun to redefine their functions, to reappraise their skills, to regard much of their past work as not good enough, and in their present ways of helping people to see vast room for improvement. They hesitated to broadcast their story until they had further tested their new techniques.

Then, too, there were available few trained persons equipped with a knowledge of both public relations and casework, able to give leadership to the caseworkers in interpretation and publicity. There is still a dearth of such trained personnel.

Most caseworkers—even before the depression— had a strong distaste for publicity, mistrusted it, saw it as a threat to their clients, tolerated it only as a necessary money-raising evil. Yet in this period of self-doubt about the quality of their work, and of unpreparedness for interpretation, the family service agencies were called upon as never before to justify their existence. If they were to survive they had, willy-nilly, to tell their story. No wonder most of them did it badly, defensively, taking refuge in technical vocabulary and in vague generalizations. Yet they did make a beginning and some excellent pieces of interpretation were produced at this time, sometimes by individual agencies, sometimes by groups of agencies.

War Prosperity Changes Public Attitudes

Difficult as were the problems of casework interpretation during the depression, they were more easily encompassed than those of the war prosperity which followed. The malignant forces of hard times gave the family agencies one strong approach to public sympathy, quite apart from that of want. It required little imagination, in a period which in some way threatened everyone, to realize that, over and above hunger and cold, people were suffering other fears, despairs, and deteriorations; and that private casework agencies might have a valuable function in preventing these emotional dangers from destroying the morale of their victims.

In the war years, however, many damages to family life disguised themselves under a mask of high wages and almost universal employment. In such ostensibly good times not only the private but the public relief agencies were challenged to justify their existence, nudged rudely by the inevitable question "What is there for you to do now that everybody has a job?" Not only caseworkers, but social workers in all branches of the profession were ready with answers. For the war had brought many acute problems: the housing of new families drawn to industrial centers by war industries; the need for care of children whose mothers worked in war plants; the increase in juvenile delinquency; and difficulties arising from lower standards—especially of those who came from rural districts—about health, sanitation, child care, and educational requirements.

The wartime social problems were not limited to newcomers. The care of children of working mothers in the regular population, for instance, has always been a challenge, and is again now that the war is over. But the war made it more urgent, since more mothers were working, and working longer hours.

Cleveland, the city of our study, shared all these problems. Its caseworkers knew well the impact of war's emotional by-products: the troubles of women, disturbed and frightened by the absence and the dangers of their menfolk; of children growing up without their fathers; of bewildered adolescents groping for their place in today's scheme of things; not to mention the confusions and mortification of many men rejected by or discharged from the armed forces before the war's end—all these taxed the wisdom and the facilities of social agencies to capacity. All agencies, except those which administer public assistance, were called upon increasingly for old and new services.

Only poverty decreased. In Cleveland, one out of every four persons in the metropolitan area had had to seek direct public assistance or work relief in the depths of the depression, as compared with one out of six for the country as a whole. In 1944 general relief was a minor problem with only 18 or 19 persons per 1,000 receiving any of the forms of public assistance; while general assistance of the type most responsive to unemployment problems of families, fell to about five persons per 1,000.[1] True, the demands upon the more permanent forms of public assistance and social security provisions, such as Aid to Dependent Children and Old Age Assistance, underwent relatively little decrease. Child dependence and neglect were still acute. New hardships, too, troubled the many salaried workers whose pay failed to parallel rising costs. And many families whose men were drafted knew privation.

Other people, free of financial need, were driven by various war pressures to seek out the private family agencies. Some of these agencies in Cleveland and elsewhere had tested the validity of casework enough during the depression to be convinced that it was a helping process good for troubled people no matter what their financial circumstances. To be sure, for some time after the establishment of public relief the private agencies continued to draw their clientele chiefly from families in precarious, if not desperate condition—families receiving public aid, or so near the edge of dependency that the slightest push of ill fortune could have toppled them into it.

FEE SERVICES

Soon, however, people in easier circumstances began to bring their troubles to the private casework

[1] According to the Research Division of the Welfare Federation of Cleveland.

agency. As a result, during the war period some 15 member agencies of the Family Service Association of America established fee services.[1] Thus anyone could have the benefit of the same skilled help which these agencies gave to the great bulk of their clients.

The development of the fee service, though new, was foreshadowed as long ago as 1922, when Mary Richmond in What Is Social Case Work? wrote:

Every month or so, some new and beneficent application of social case work to human welfare—often from an entirely unexpected quarter—comes to my attention. Sometimes the new development is far removed from the types of service in which case work originated. One of these, for example, comes in the private practice of physicians and psychiatrists, who, after seeing what case work can do in their free clinics, are seeking the services of case workers for their well-to-do patients. How rapidly social case work will develop a private practice of its own cannot be predicted, but it should be evident from the examples given in this book that the skill here described can be utilized quite as well in the homes of the rich as in those of the poor, that, in the one as in the other, personality can be thwarted and retarded, developed and enriched.[2]

The 15 agencies which have in recent years established a fee service, have varied in their ways of setting it up; in their ways of making it known; and in the boldness with which they departed from their

[1] The Jewish Family Service of New York was the first family agency to inaugurate a fee service. In 1942 it set up a separate experimental office, the Consultation Center, which it publicized in every available channel—the newspapers, radio, and by special interpretation to groups and individuals. Because of the success of this demonstration, early in 1946 the agency extended fee service in all its district offices to those who could pay for it, but it still continued the Consultation Center.

[2] Russell Sage Foundation, New York, 1922, p. 221.

long-entrenched tradition, and from the public's notion of what they did. In Cleveland, for instance, the largest casework agency—the Family Service Association—established its fee service on a permissive basis: anyone who wished to pay might do so. On the other hand, the Jewish Family Service Association of Cleveland decided to charge everyone—except those who could not afford to pay.[1] Today family service agencies look on the payment of fees as a part of treatment for those who can afford to pay.

Some agencies publicized this new step widely. Others, fearing perhaps that their contributors needed a slower weaning from habitual concepts about family agencies, adopted an almost hush-hush policy about fee charging. They confined their interpretation at first to special referral sources, and only gradually widened their audience.

The establishment of the fee service was a big stride toward democratizing the philosophy of the one-time charity agencies, now become casework agencies. They began to climb into a class of service which, like medicine, was needed in certain situations by all kinds of people, whether or not they could afford to pay. As the Cleveland Family Service Association's annual report for 1945 comments, "The idea that the family agency deals only with the misfits of society is out. There are times in the lives of most people when a caseworker could steer them through a troubled period and prevent disaster costly to the community."[2]

[1] Other Cleveland casework agencies which charge or accept fees are: the Cleveland Guidance Center, the Children's Service, the Youth Bureau, and the Planned Parenthood Association.

[2] Today—Family Service. Annual Report, 1945.

To be sure, only a small percentage of the country's casework agencies have begun to accept pay for their services. Most of their clients continue to come from families where illness, unemployment, or other distress pyramid the financial as well as emotional strain. But the use of a family service agency by those who can pay makes it just so much more acceptable and useful to those who cannot. This wider use tends to remove what many potential clients consider the stigma of charity, as well as the sting of self-reproach for needing professional help.

Changes in Agency Names

Apart from the practice of fee charging, casework agencies have shown another democratic trend. This appears in their new titles. Of the 234 member agencies of the Family Service Association of America, only five at the present writing retain in their titles the words "charity" and "relief"—words widely current only a decade ago. Many agencies outside the Association do still cling to the word "charity," on the strength of its good, original meaning. More generally, however, the casework field believes that either of these words in a title tends to limit an agency's usefulness; that many people who would balk at "charity" or "relief" would ask for "service," feeling in this no loss of personal dignity. Many children's agencies, too, have changed their names. They now tend to prefer some such title as "children's center," or "children's bureau," to the old "home," "orphanage," "humane society," or "society for the prevention of cruelty to children."

A title may be either a good or a bad instrument of public relations.

INTERPRETATION OF SERVICES FOR CHILDREN

The family service agencies were pushed harder and earlier toward interpretation than were the other casework agencies. The depression did not goad the child-care agencies, for example, to defend their right to survive. True, it cut into their support, but only because money was hard to get, not because the public challenged their value.

Their hardest pressure came later, during the war. Then the need was not so much for financing that part of their service which the public understood—food and shelter—as for staff to provide casework services to children in their own homes, for more good foster homes for children who needed substitute parents, and for day care for children of mothers who worked in war plants.

The last two needs—and especially the need for foster homes—were the ones which the children's agencies brought before the public. They found it comparatively easy to make people see how the disruptive forces of the war upon families were harming children. Many child-care agencies—sometimes individually, sometimes in collaboration with others, and, as in Cleveland, with newspapers—carried on successful campaigns both for foster homes and for day-care programs. Unfortunately, even these told the public little about the casework which is essential to happy foster home placement, and basic also in helping parents to use the day-care programs.

OTHER CASEWORK SERVICES

As for other fields of social work in which casework is practiced—medical social service, casework in institutions, in unions, in industries, in schools—few marked efforts to secure general public understanding were stimulated either by the depression or the war. But the growing use of casework in these fields could not have been brought about or kept alive without interpretation. For the most part, however, this has been specialized, inside interpretation to staff and boards or administrative groups which finance the service.

Perhaps the greatest problems of acceptance and effective use of casework and of interpretation, both during the depression and the war, lay in the public welfare fields which have long used personal service, but where casework by professionally trained workers still had to inch its way in. For instance, in public assistance (the largest unit of personal service); in courts; or in various institutions. All of these—both because of a dearth of trained caseworkers and a failure to realize that these services require special casework skills—have been staffed for the most part by persons without casework training. The use of trained caseworkers in such settings varies from community to community, and within communities.[1]

CASEWORK'S PUBLIC RELATIONS AFTER THE WAR

The war's end brought new problems and revived some old ones: unemployment, strikes, the struggle

[1] The New York State Social Welfare Law, for example, makes it possible to give casework services even to those who do not need financial aid. But New York City's interpretation of the Law, at present, does not provide for such services except to persons who also get financial assistance.

with reduced incomes because of the stoppage of over-time pay, the soaring cost of living. And the scores of troubles of returning veterans and their families. And the pressures upon families whose men did not return.

This reshuffling of social anxieties has required of casework new kinds of help, and help in new places. It has challenged the caseworkers to seek effective ways of letting people know where they can get the help they need; and in other ways to establish sounder and more widespread public relations—and this at a time when there is an acute shortage of trained caseworkers.

As a result the casework field is confronted with something like a riddle: why, especially now when the demand for caseworkers is so great that it cannot be met for years, when thousands of caseworkers and casework administrators have been drawn off into war-created or postwar services—the various departments of the American National Red Cross and Veterans Administration Centers, for instance—why, at this time should agencies and councils of social agencies go to the trouble and expense of spreading information about casework?

Some agencies have indeed decided against a program of interpretation, thinking that to bring more clients to their doors than they could give adequate service to would be no kindness to the clients, and a bad public relations policy. Other agencies, without coming to any such definite decision, have on much the same basis let the matter slide.

There seems, however, to be a strong urge in the casework field to make known the values and uses of casework and to deal with whatever new pressures this information may bring. Caseworkers tend to feel that casework services are the right of persons needing them, and that the whole task of increasing provision for an intelligent use of such services must be faced. They feel that the relations between caseworkers and those who work with them in helping clients— doctors, teachers, judges, lawyers, ministers, for instance, and all other referral sources—need to be improved. They feel that if the bottleneck is lack of personnel then special attention must be given to interpretation in recruiting personnel and students for schools of social work. They feel that these schools—which consider casework basic to all social work—should make clear and vivid to potential students just what casework is and does, and what it requires of and offers to its practitioners.

The Limitations of Casework and Their Effect on Public Understanding

Any discussion of public understanding of casework must keep in mind some of the hurdles set up by the status of casework itself. Because for our study we selected a community where both casework and public understanding rank perhaps well above the average, and because we select for illustration this community's outstanding examples of ventures in public relations, we run the danger of presenting both casework and its interpretation as more advanced than in general they are.

The reader of this book, then, would do well to remember certain limitations of casework which must affect its public relations: That casework, for example, covers only a small part of the need for it. That, as in any branch of any new profession, its quality is uneven, ranging from first rate to feeble. That countless persons who might profit by it will long be reluctant to seek it—out of shame or embarrassment at having to ask outsiders for help with problems of personality or of family relationships, or because they think of it as something only for the destitute. That caseworkers see no immediate likelihood of curing or preventing the bulk of social and emotional strains which put people in need of their services—any more than doctors see an immediate possibility of curing or preventing cancer.

For a long time casework will be limited to persons driven to it by some fairly acute inner need, or guided to it by some information service, and limited, too, by the casework agency's capacity in both personnel and knowledge.

New Thresholds

This knowledge, however, is growing. Caseworkers have learned much about human relationships, and about the components which make for more satisfactory family living. They have learned less about the ways of sharing their knowledge with their public or getting their services understood.

Casework provides no facile solutions to the countless kaleidoscopic puzzles of human relationships. And the art or business of public relations for social work, in general, and casework in particular, is still in its youth. The specialists both in casework and in public relations are concerned with the practical steps toward wider usefulness and better understanding, and, to this end, are asking many questions:

Whose task is casework interpretation? What is the individual caseworker's responsibility? How best can each agency present its work? How, in view of casework's many new venturings and of the unmet demands for its services, can agencies join forces in reaching the public? What public or publics do they wish to reach? What do they wish these publics to know about casework? What does the public now know, think, and feel about casework? What confusions and misconceptions about casework are most hampering to its users or possible users? What is the relation between the quality of casework and public understanding of casework? What is there in the *content* of casework which might be passed on to a fairly general public? How have the various channels of publicity been effectively used? And how, through further interpretation, can casework push forward its frontiers?

Questions like these are springing up in every field of casework—public and private, local and national. They concern, too, the schools of social work, both in the recruiting and in the training of students to fill the growing demands for caseworkers. Although many of the answers are yet to be found, the questioning is a healthy sign, because the range of casework's usefulness and its potentialities for further development depend upon the extent and quality of public understanding.

CHAPTER II

THE CASEWORKER'S TASK
IN PUBLIC RELATIONS

PEOPLE learn about casework in various ways: through the caseworker; through the client who has used casework services and tells others about it; through persons in the community—for instance, teachers, doctors, ministers—who have seen what it has done for clients; through planned interpretation and publicity, by individual agencies and councils of social agencies; through community chest campaigns.

But all interpretation stems back to the caseworker—to what she is and does, and how she thinks and feels and talks about her work. Though she cannot—and should not—be expected to carry an agency's public relations program, she is the taproot from which all public understanding grows. The nature and quality of her services determine what the client says. They predicate what the agency spokesman—executive, board member, public relations specialist—can say and the conviction with which he can speak.

The caseworker, however, is more than a source of interpretation. She is herself an interpreter. Consciously or unconsciously, she is always creating feeling and opinion. The quality of her interpretation varies, according to her natural ability to carry on a give-and-take relationship with other people; according to the specialized guidance she gets, and the thought she contributes to the task; and according to her own understanding of casework.

All too often it is only in relation to the client that she develops her skill as an interpreter. Here she has had direction and training. A capacity to understand the needs and interests of her client, and to make clear to him in what ways her agency can help him, is of the essence of good casework.

No part of her professional training, however, has compelled her to acquire analogous skill in wider interpretation. Few schools of social work provide courses in this field; and when she gets a job, the pressure of her caseload and the concern with improving her casework techniques so crowd her day that she finds little time to develop what interest and ability she might have in the field of community relations, and she gets little or no guidance in this direction.

THE CASEWORKER'S RESPONSIBILITY FOR INTERPRETATION

Despite the lack of training or opportunity for training in public relations, the casework field is beginning to require an ability to interpret as part of the caseworker's equipment.

The Social Case Work Council of the National Social Welfare Assembly in 1946 issued a Report on Classification of Positions in Voluntary Case Work Agencies. This report lists some responsibility for interpretation among the duties of everyone from supervisor to case aide.

38

As for the family service field, a report of the personnel committee of the Family Service Association of America[1] goes farther and is more specific in describing the public relations qualifications and responsibilities of casework personnel. Such requirements range from "ability to establish and maintain good working relationships with persons in the community in relation to cases under care and interpretation of case work through such contacts," for beginning caseworkers, to the more complicated responsibility of a district secretary, who "should be able to win the confidence of district committees of laymen and of other professionals in the case work and allied fields. He should be able to interpret case work in uncomplicated language and to accept the validity of other points of view. While it would be helpful for him to have skill in writing or making speeches about case work, it is not essential that he possess this quality himself provided he senses it in others and fosters its development in his staff."

As for positions beyond these—casework supervisors, consultants, assistant executives, and finally executives—the responsibility for community relations continues to increase. The executive, for instance, must be able not only to interpret to boards but to "interpret the agency through writing, talks, community contacts, and other publicity methods . . ." and is responsible for "interpretation and publicity directly related to community understanding of

[1] Family Service Association of America, Classifications of Professional Positions in Private Family Agencies. Prepared by Subcommittee on Classifications in Private Family Agencies, Committee on Family Social Work Personnel, New York, 1946.

agency and community education regarding the forces that strengthen or destroy family life."

Thus the importance of interpretation as one responsibility of every professional worker in the casework field, and the place of interpretation as an essential function of the casework agency get, so to speak, official recognition. They are, however, more honored in the breach than in the observance.

Experiment with Conversations

In Cleveland, as elsewhere, caseworkers are beginning to ask themselves, "How good are we as purveyors of information about our jobs? Can't we find some better methods than the groping trial-and-error of our present ways?"

To this end, some of Cleveland's caseworkers undertook to study themselves as individual interpreters. In three agencies, the Family Service Association, the Jewish Family Service Association, and the Cuyahoga County Relief Bureau, a public agency, caseworkers agreed to record their conversations about their work, both in connection with their job, and in off-the-job contacts. In the two private agencies members of the clerical staff also participated in the experiment. In one agency some volunteers also took part.

These conversations were not to be forced. Only those which happened spontaneously were to be recorded. By way of preparation, however, the groups discussed the last conversations they had had with outsiders about their work. They considered such matters as what they had told; what questions they had been asked; how they had answered them; what interested their listeners; where interest had flagged; which questions were hard to answer and which were easy; how they thought they rated as interpreters; in what ways they thought they were well equipped and in what ways unprepared to tell about their work; and how they *felt* when they tried to talk about it.

It is significant that both in these preliminary discussions of past conversations, and in the later ones, the caseworkers said it was comparatively easy to tell about their work or the work of their agency when they were consulting with someone about a particular case, whether the conversation had to do with getting information or advice, or was only the routine reporting back to the referral source as to how the agency had been of service to the client referred.

On the other hand, many if not most of the caseworkers found even casual explanations to outsiders difficult. "It's odd," said one, "we can let a client know how we can help him. We can explain what we are doing to a person interested in a particular case, like a teacher, or a minister, or a doctor. But let anyone outside, even a minister or a teacher or a doctor ask—say at a dinner party—'Just what *is* casework?' or 'Just what do you *do*?' and we get that drowning sensation." "Oh," sighed another, a visitor in a public agency, "Oh, to be able to settle that question by saying, 'I'm a dishwasher at Duke's Dive' or 'I teach English at Whitmer High' or 'I'm a second line girl at the Roxy!' People know these occupations but a Public Health and Welfare Visitor is an oddity."

This feeling of helplessness is by no means peculiar to caseworkers in Cleveland. Indeed, it is much less marked there than in places less active in public relations. The writer of this report has for some years carried on similar experiments with groups of students, and with one group of executives, who in turn tried them with their staffs. In all these experiments, the prevailing reaction has been that of reluctance if not a "drowning sensation" when confronted with the need to inform "outsiders" about casework.

A good many of the Cleveland caseworkers who took part in this project, in answer to the question, "What did you say the last time anyone asked you what you did?" had replied effectively and specifically with some variant of "I told them how we had helped a particular family," or "I said, 'Well, this is what I did today.'" And many of them had with ease and confidence given a clear picture of their work—or some part of it—in simple, non-technical English.

But even in Cleveland, where much excellent interpretation has been carried on by individual agencies and by the Welfare Federation, most of the answers in these preliminary reports were defensive. They ranged from a vague, "We help people out of a jam" to the evasive, "Oh, I never talk about my work outside office hours." They included—and these replies are not exceptional—such statements as: "I suppose you think social workers try to manage other people's lives for them; well, we're not like that"; and "It took me two years to learn my job. How do you expect me to tell you what it is in ten minutes?" One caseworker reported that during her vacation when people asked her what she did she said she was a teacher, "to avoid argument." Another reported that she avoided talking about her work because it made her lose her temper. Another said, "I find myself trying to avoid the effort of explaining . . . it seems easier to argue over misconceptions because at least misconceptions are a starting point." Several reported that they saved up amusing incidents for dinner conversations, having decided it was almost impossible to interest their listeners in social work in any other way.

These evasive and defensive attitudes were no index to the quality of the casework of the individuals who expressed them, many of whom rank high in their profession. What is more, many of the others who had given fairly good answers had felt the same defensiveness and the same befuddlement as to what they wished to say.

Why should this be? What makes it so difficult for the average caseworker to tell the average layman about her work?

REASONS FOR THE CASEWORKER'S PERPLEXITIES

The answers are various. The present nature of casework gives us some. Its history provides others. The attitudes of the caseworkers, which in turn grow out of the nature and history of, and training for, their work, furnish others still. And the experience and attitudes of the public, interwoven, of course, with all the foregoing, fill in with the rest.

Perhaps it is the wide range of casework which makes it perplexing to describe. It has so many facets, so many depths, so many earthy practicalities, so many subtleties. It has different meanings to the

43

different persons it helps. It lacks an easily recognizable focus. The question "Just what do you do?" brings leaping into the caseworker's mind a host of answers, no one of which is a clear, complete answer. Yet she must make a swift decision. She can hardly say, "My field is the whole range of human behavior," though it is. She must decide in a split second whether to skim off some easily acceptable service—such as the visiting housekeeper, or vocational guidance—or whether to dredge deeper, fathoming the psychological waters of personality treatment; whether to tell a case story, and what case story or what part of it to tell. She has to select from her experience some particular matter, to interest her particular interlocutor. She has to decide how much to tell, how much to leave untold.

And against this embarrassment of riches, she often has a worse hurdle: a poverty of conviction in her own attitudes. It is not that she lacks belief in the value of casework, or even in her own ability to do it reasonably well. (Though occasionally she does lack these too.) Rather she is laboriously aware of the limitations of casework, of the inevitably slow pace of helping people one by one on a trail which may in many instances be long.

She knows, too, that casework is still new, with much still to learn. She is aware that the agencies which do casework have, many of them, changed the emphasis in their functions only in recent years; and that the public still tends to identify casework agencies with their relief-giving past. Or, if she happens to be a caseworker in a relief agency, she is aware that the public knows little of the philosophy of today's relief work and she fears they might not like it if they did know.

In short, she expects a hostile public, and braces herself for antagonisms which are as often imagined as real. She suffers a handicap common among her clients: insecurity.

One of the ways in which this insecurity showed itself in the experimental conversations was the effect of community criticism upon the caseworker. If someone said, "I sent a family to an agency, and all they got was a runaround," or "Mrs. X went to the Family Welfare and all that happened was talk, talk, talk," the caseworker's reaction was all too often apologetic, argumentative, or otherwise defensive. Only a few reported that in such cases they could say easily without suffering a sense of guilt, "Yes, social work still lacks adequate organization," or "Well, that sounds like bad casework." Or "Sometimes the talk, talk, talk, is a way of letting someone unload troubles."

Unlike the doctor, who does not go about wringing his hands because his profession has so far failed to find a way to prevent the common cold, who takes failure to cure as often inevitable, the caseworker tends to feel that, with every clumsy or bad piece of casework, every failure of society to prevent conditions which bring people to agencies like hers, it is for *her* conscience that the bell tolls.

This sense of social responsibility has led to many good social reforms. One would not want it weakened. Well guided, rather, so that it should help and not hinder the understanding and use of casework and of other kinds of social work as well.

Oddly enough, the very preparation which has made the caseworker a better caseworker has contributed to her timidity with the public. In the course of supervised, disciplined training, in which she learned to apply professional concepts productively in helping people, she had also to slough off or uproot many of her own attitudes—a difficult, often painful process. She discovered that her work, chosen out of sympathy with distressed and troubled people, and a wish to make life better for them, requires much more than kindliness, knowledge, industry, and sympathy. These, of course, she must have. But the training which gave her a new quality and depth of understanding also required her to give up the luxury of identifying herself emotionally either with her client or with those who contribute the funds for her work.

Remembering her struggle with her own attitudes, she finds it hard to believe that the public will easily accept her new philosophy. Having spent much time acquiring methods of helping people, she tends to believe that she must explain these methods. She feels pressed to tell, too, some of the knowledge she has acquired of the workings of the human mind and spirit, and how each human being's inner world may affect his actions and reactions to individual as well as to social pressures, and how, in turn, these pressures remake his inner world. And she wants to tell how these pressures affect not only people with money troubles, but people in every economic class; and how casework now offers itself to those who wish to pay for it, as well as to those who cannot. She tends either to understate or to oversell what casework can do.

Remembering her pretrained ideas and attitudes, no wonder she often begins to tell her questioner the things casework is *not* rather than what it is. Or that sometimes to counteract her own sense of smallness as measured against a big task she rather clumsily dwells upon the importance of a caseworker's methods and skills.

The Prevailing Problems in the Conversations

The following were the most common difficulties reported not only by the Cleveland caseworkers who took part in this experiment in conversation but also by those in other groups:

How to choose what to tell.

How to talk about casework without using technical language.

How to know when to stop.

How to keep a story from getting top-heavy with scientific information which the public isn't ready to take.

How to make representative rather than extraordinary cases sound interesting. How to turn a desire to hear about abnormal and extreme cases to an interest in representative cases.

How to find a representative case.

How to overcome the attitude that persons who ask help from social agencies are weaklings or otherwise inferior.

How to convey what is involved in casework without sounding self-important and without oversimplification.

How to overcome antagonism, prejudices, and misinformation.

47

As for specific questions which the caseworkers found difficult to answer the following were those most commonly reported:

What do you do that a minister, doctor, or lawyer doesn't do?

Isn't your work just patching things up?

How do you measure your accomplishments?

In what percentage of your cases are people really rehabilitated?

How can anyone so young, inexperienced in life, and unmarried deal with marriage difficulties and troubles between parents and children?

Don't you have to be hard-boiled to be a social worker?

Isn't that work awfully depressing?

Why can't normal people work out their own difficulties? Aren't you simply fostering dependency?

Doesn't social work take away the incentive to work?

What good does it do just to talk to people?

Why should private agencies exist when we are taxed for public relief?

Why should we be taxed for relief when everyone has a job?

Isn't it unpleasant to know that your having a job depends on other people having troubles?

What is the policy of your agency about the Fair Employment Practices Bill (or other pending legislation)?

And the most frequently asked and most difficult question of them all: *"Just what is casework?"*

WHAT PEOPLE LIKE TO HEAR

Besides listing the questions difficult to answer some of the caseworkers made a note of the things people liked to hear. Of these the most common was the illustrative case story, "a story showing how we

actually helped some individual person or family."
Others reported an interest in "psychiatric concepts
of behavior, especially those which seem related to the
problems in the questioner's own family or among his
friends." And again, "People want to hear about
clients for whom they have natural sympathy—children, old people, people they can *like*." And "They
like to hear the simple everyday things of life, the
nice things you are doing for children. They like to
feel that all is being taken care of and that there are
no poor people suffering today." And one reported,
"They like to hear about national organizations doing
things on a big scale, helping large numbers of people."

On the other hand, several reported that "People
want to hear the wrong things—amusing stories
about clients." Or, "They want to hear things which
fit in with their own political ideas." Or, "They don't
really want to hear anything. They just ask out of
politeness and listen for the same reason." But comments such as these were the exception.

What the Caseworkers Learned from the Experiment

In discussing their attempts to tell people about
their work most of the caseworkers agreed that they
were inadequately equipped for this task. Apart from
a need for knowledge of how to deal with their own
attitudes, and how to develop greater skill in interpretation, they found they needed a better knowledge
of their own agency—its work as a whole, its accomplishments and needs; and how its work dovetailed

into the needs of the rest of the community. They reported, too, a need of more exchange of experience with other workers both in their own and in other agencies, so that they would have a wider field than their own caseload to draw upon for illustrative material.

"But most of all," one caseworker summed it up, "we need more confidence. Confidence in ourselves, and in our agency and in social work as a whole, so that we can give others confidence that what we do is good and useful and necessary."

The conversations which the caseworkers recorded after discussion of their difficulties and what they wished to accomplish when they talked about their work, were much more successful than the haphazard ones before the experiment. They varied, of course, in the quality of interestingness; for beyond all earnest inner conviction and even training in interpretation, people do vary in their ability to interest others.

Many, however, found that by using the same kind of imagination and awareness as they used with their clients, they could pick from their experience material which interested the persons they talked with. They found they did not have to cover the whole field of their experience, but could tell some small part of it quite simply and without retreating into professional jargon; and could gauge how much to tell by the interest they aroused. They found they could be content to say, "I don't know," when they didn't, without making the other person feel, or, for that matter, without themselves feeling, that not to know was a felony. They could say, "I'll find out about that if I can, and let you know later."

And they could tell a case story—though this was not easy—without beginning with the childhood of the parent of the client and working their laborious way up through adolescence, marriage, and child bearing; they could select only that part of a story which illustrated some particular problem or service.

Some of them found the experience so profitable that they tried and reported several conversations. Others were less successful, and some did not succeed at all. But most of them did make progress. In fact, some who in reviewing past conversations reported the greatest difficulties had surprising successes in subsequent ones. Or not so surprising either. Any good caseworker has the potential ability to tell about her work, for this requires some of the very qualities which go to make her a good caseworker: sensitiveness to the interest of others, and a quiet inner knowledge that her work is valuable.

Experiments with conversations have a value not only in themselves, but a wider use. The demand which every caseworker must constantly meet, of having to tell chance inquirers what she does, can form a basis of staff training for interpretation; and for interpretation not only through individual contacts, but in more formal public relations projects. In learning what interests people one by one, and how to interest them more skillfully, the caseworker lays a foundation for being able to hold the attention of groups of people, whether in meetings or in the writing of bulletins and reports; or in the wider ranges of the newspaper and radio.

Suppose we look at a few reports of effective conversations.

CHAPTER III

CONVERSATION PIECES

THE conversations chosen for report in this chapter include many questions commonly asked. The ingredients of the answers, too, are typical. Yet each of these conversations is highly individual, with a flavor of its own. Little technical verbiage muffles what the caseworker has to say. Little slumping into the lazy cliché or leaning back on formula separates her and her interlocutor. In one or two instances the caseworkers had rather rough going to get the listener's interest or approval. Usually the quality of their knowledge and their confidence in their profession showed them an accessible path.

Our first report illustrates the ease with which a group accepted a new and, to them, strange idea of an agency's work when it was presented with simple, unpretentious conviction by the caseworker. The talk, which spread over several hours, is telescoped here. Most of the persiflage and pleasant irrelevancies, and some of the pertinent discussion, too, are omitted. The abbreviation makes the accomplishment seem faster than it was, but an attempt is made to report accurately the gist and, so far as possible, the words of the conversation.

TABLE TALK[1]

The insurance man came late to our table at the dinner for Community Fund volunteers. Introductions went

[1] Reported by Lillian G. Greenberg, caseworker, Jewish Family Service Association of Cleveland.

around. He was respectful to the lady interne, polite to the two settlement workers, jovial to the telephone operator. He sat down next to me and after some conversation asked just what my organization—the Jewish Family Service Association—did.

I began to tell him that we were interested in families, in the problems families had, such as the troubles between parents and children or between husbands and wives.

"Do you mean," he interrupted jokingly, "that I contribute to the Fund so that people who are going to get a divorce anyway can call each other names in your office?"

We all laughed, but I tried to answer seriously. "Sometimes there is a divorce anyway. It's not our purpose to force people who are unhappy together to live together. But sometimes, through the help we are equipped to give them, they straighten out their difficulties."

"But why should a *philanthropic* agency do that? I don't mind giving money to help the needy. But if they have enough money or if they don't neglect their children—"

"Suppose," I said, "that you think of the agency as a community service, not only for people in financial need but for anybody. That is, you contribute so that the service can exist. You, yourself, should feel free to use it."

"Who? *Me!!*"

"You sound awfully vehement. Of course I hope you'll always be able to meet whatever problems arise in your life. But people do have problems they can't settle with their own resources, don't they? Or they may have resources within themselves but not know how to use them. This is something our agency helps people do."

"Well, I certainly don't think of a Fund agency as something for *me* to use."

I asked him if he had hospitalization insurance and if he had ever used it.

"Not so far." He knocked wood.

"Do you mind others using it?"

"Of course not. That's why they take out insurance."

"Still, in a way, they are being hospitalized at your expense. And you would be at theirs, if you used it."

He grinned. "I get your point. You're comparing hospitalization and the services your agency gives."

"In a way, yes."

"Well, it's a new idea all right. But let's say, just for instance, that I'm a potential customer for your agency. What have you got to sell? In other words, what could you do for *me?*"

"You know yourself better than I know you. Perhaps *you* can suggest some way in which our agency might be helpful to you."

"Well, I'm over twenty-one, in good health and doing well in insurance. I have friends and influence people. Now," he laughed, "can you get me a raise?"

I laughed too. "Do you think you deserve a raise?"

"Sure."

"Have you asked for one?"

He had not.

"Well," I tried to match his bantering tone, and yet to say what I thought, "if you feel that not being able to get a raise or to ask for one is a problem, or if you feel unhappy in your job, either about accomplishment or your relationships to other people, we could help."

"Of course you're kidding?"

"No. Just illustrating one phase of our work."

Still facetious, he asked if I could get his brother-in-law a job.

"Our agency doesn't do that. But your brother-in-law could use other community resources, which you and he are both paying for, through your contributions to the Community Fund."

Now the conversation became general.

"Don't people feel shy coming to your agency for help?" asked the telephone operator.

I said that some did. "But not those who think of the agency as belonging to them, and the services as something they're entitled to."

"The way they feel," said one of the settlement workers, "about using a community recreation service, or going to the Y. The Community Fund helps support those, too."

"That's different," said the telephone operator. "But to go to an agency like Miss Greenberg's—well it would be admitting I wasn't bright enough to manage my own problems."

"I'd feel that way, too," said the interne. "As if I ought to be able to work them out for myself."

"Still, using our agency is like going to a doctor because of a stomach-ache. One may diagnose one's own pain as indigestion and take a laxative. But if it's appendicitis the laxative is the worst possible treatment. People can make just as serious mistakes trying to cure their emotional ills. In both instances you'd want a specialist."

"There's a clerk in my office," said the insurance salesman. "He's a case. Sneaky. Can't get along with anybody. Could you do something with a person like that?"

"If he came to us for help, we'd try to discover what had made him that kind of person, and we'd try to help him toward a happier adjustment within himself. And also in relation to other people."

"Well, that would be worth my contribution to the Fund! The man isn't Jewish, though."

I told him about the Family Service Association, which offers the same kinds of help to non-Jewish clients.

"In all the years I've been contributing to the Fund and collecting for it," said the telephone operator, "no one ever told me anything about the agencies except that they helped people in trouble. I always thought trouble meant financial trouble."

"So did I," said the interne. "Do people from middle or well-to-do classes ever come to you?"

"From all classes, occupations and professions."

"Not professions!"

"Yes, we've been working with doctors' and dentists' families. And frequently professional people refer their clients or patients to us." And I explained that because we want people to feel that anyone can use us, we charge fees, on a sliding scale, according to income.

The insurance man approved that idea. "People in my class would be more likely to use your services if they could pay." The telephone operator asked if the Family Service Association also charged fees. I told her that people who wished to pay for their services could do so.

The program now began, interrupting our conversation. At the end of the evening, the insurance man said he was glad we had sat at the same table, because he had never thought of social agencies as I presented them. He liked the idea of services available to the whole community. It gave him a good, new, selling point, raising money for the Fund. He thought the things I had told should be made known to the general public. Personally, he felt proud that the city had such fine agencies and that anyone could use them.

As we parted, he returned to his joking tone. "Who knows," he said, "some day I may come in and let you work on me. To find out why I can't get a raise."

The next conversation, chosen as an example of the good use made of a casual, almost accidental opportunity to talk about casework, was done so naturally and with such implicit respect for the clients of the agency that the listeners, feeling a kinship with them, began to tell of their own trouble. And this conversation, as the concluding paragraphs indicate, proved but the first of a series.

CONVERSATION IN A BUTCHER SHOP[1]

The Handels'[2] grocery and butcher shop is a sociable place. Neighbors exchange their news and world problems see-saw over the counter.

One day when I chanced to be the only customer in the store Mrs. Handel asked me, "What is that house down the street? We see you and other ladies going in and out of there so busily."

I told her it was a family service office of the Associated Charities.[3]

"Surely," Mr. Handel said with a note of criticism, "no one needs relief these days. Jobs are plentiful."

"You're partly right about that," I agreed. "People don't so often need bread and butter now, though there are exceptions. But we help in other ways too. Families—especially these days—have lots of worries and heartaches and confusions. Sickness still crops up to complicate family life. In our office we see many people in whose families there is mental or physical illness."

Mr. and Mrs. Handel exchanged glances.

"*Mental* illness?" Mrs. Handel asked.

"Often," I said. And I told them about two boys—thirteen and fifteen—whose mother had had nervous breakdowns and how we supported the family through their bad times, arranging hospital care for the mother and finding someone to look out for the boys, who otherwise would have been stranded.

Mrs. Handel looked questioningly at her husband. After a moment he half nodded, as if it was safe to say what was in their minds.

"We have a sick son just out of the Army," she said.

[1] Reported by Catherine Bennett, at the time with the Family Service Association of Cleveland.

[2] Not the real name.

[3] Now the Family Service Association of Cleveland.

57

"It's sleeping sickness. He doesn't want anyone to come into his room except his grandmother. Dr. Z, the well-known doctor, is on his case."

She stopped and then added, "You see *we* are taking care of our *own* problem."

"It's good to help ourselves," I said. "Many people do. But some families aren't lucky enough to have grandmothers like yours or doctors like Dr. Z. People often don't know where to turn when trouble hits home."

"Yes," said Mr. Handel, "it could be like that."

"Our staff," I said, "in one way is like Dr. Z and Grandmother Handel. Someone to turn to. Our workers are trained in social work—the job of helping people in trouble. It is not that we 'do' for people so much as that we help them to do for themselves."

For a moment the Handels were as quiet as the cans on their shelves. Then they began to speak again of their son, telling of his illness, their anxieties and hopes for him.

They stopped as a customer came into the store. Mr. Handel paused to say, "We never thought about some of those things you said. I guess it isn't just shiftless people who have troubles and need help."

This was the first of many conversations, sometimes alone with the Handels, oftener when other customers were present. Because of these talks, a good many persons came to know about the work of our agency, especially perhaps about one phase of it; for, since this was a food store, it was natural to tell of the things we do to help families plan meals and shop wisely.

One day I brought the Handels some copies of our pamphlet, Family Affairs, which carried an article "Gremlins in the Budget," about wise shopping.

On my next visit Mrs. Handel said, "You know that pamphlet? I've been giving it out. It's wonderful. Beef hearts are going fine! Now couldn't you do as much for calves brains?"

58

In both the Family Service Association and the Jewish Family Service Association, not only case-workers but members of the clerical staff also took part in this experiment with conversations. Both these agencies feel that the clerical worker as well as the caseworker is a pivot of opinion, and in a position to gain or lose friends for the agency and invite or repel the use of its services. The conversations reported by members of the clerical staffs gave evidence of both competence and confidence. Indeed some clerical workers seemed to have less difficulty in giving a good account of their agency's work than did some of the caseworkers.

In one instance an office manager did such a good job describing her agency's work to an equipment salesman, that at the end of the conversation he said he wished he might have known of such a social agency a few years ago—he could have used one himself. In another instance the switchboard operator was responsible for establishing excellent working relations between her agency and the Masonic Lodge to which her husband belonged. He had suggested, when the nervous and upset widow of a member wanted to place one of her children in the Masonic home, that this was the kind of case his wife's agency took care of. Several members questioned what a "relief agency" could possibly do in such a case; but he convinced them it was not just a relief agency, and persuaded them to try; and the results were so good that the lodge has since called upon the agency to help in other cases.

The following account of a clerical worker's conversation presents the work of the Family Service Association with a natural, simple directness.

Conversation with a Bank Manager[1]

When I opened a savings account at the Cleveland Trust Bank recently, the manager, noticing the name Associated Charities[2] on my check, asked if we were still busy at our office. I said we were busier than at any time in our history. (Having been with the agency almost ten years and having noted the increase of cases I felt qualified to make this statement.) He looked surprised and said he wondered why, since so many people were now employed and did not need financial assistance. I replied that we no longer carried many relief situations, though we did supplement some budgets—for instance, a serviceman's allotment; or where a family was large and the wage earner was not earning enough to take care of the family's entire needs. But I explained that this was only done in cases where there were other problems which needed attention by a trained case-worker—neglect of the children, for instance; or health problems; or the mother working and the children being left unsupervised; or cases where there were marital difficulties.

He became quite interested and asked numerous questions about the work of the agency and what the procedure was in many of the cases.

I am not a trained worker and only a stenographer in a branch office, but I explained to the best of my ability. He said that many people have the feeling that the agency—carrying the name Associated Charities—is still giving relief, and that there is little understanding of the real work being done. He asked what we did with children in homes where there was real neglect. I explained that such cases were referred to a children's agency for placement in foster homes, to day nurseries, or orphanage homes.

[1] Reported by Mrs. Margaret Becker, stenographer, Jackson District Office.

[2] This conversation took place before the recent change of the agency's name to Family Service Association of Cleveland.

He asked what was done in case of marital difficulties. I explained that the caseworker tried to make one or both parties see and understand what was causing the difficulty; that we did not advocate separations; but if adjustments could not be made and either or both parties decided that separation was the only way out, then help was given in working through divorce or whatever plan was desired. I also explained that many women came to us for help with budget planning, often because a family had become involved in debt and could not seem to find a way out of their difficulty.

He kept me talking to him for almost three-quarters of an hour. Then he seemed to have a much better understanding of the agency's work and policies and thanked me for talking with him.

The above conversations had to do with the private family casework field. Now, we turn to conversations in the field of public welfare.

Here we might expect the tone to be controversial with holdover attitudes from the depression years. In those days the subject of relief in almost any talk was likely to precipitate argument, if not invective, with both the "reliefers" and the social workers who urged more generous and more skillfully administered relief as targets for attack. Small wonder that public welfare workers and social workers in general should, during that period, have become defensive or even timid; or that even after the passage of some fifteen years, many of them should still doubt the public's readiness for high standards of public help.

The few conversations reported from the public welfare field in our experiment tend to show a greater readiness for such standards than the social workers expected. Some of these conversations—like the two following—grew out of a chance acquaintance with a family or individual in need of help.

CONVERSATION WITH A CIVIL SERVICE EMPLOYE[1]

Mr. X, who has been for many years connected with Cleveland public service units and concerned with taxes, told me of the plight of the old lady next door, who had cancer and little money. I described the County Nursing Home.

He obviously had in mind the great size and impersonality of public poor farms for he asked how many patients were in the County Nursing Home. When I told him it cared for only 175, he asked the per capita cost of running it. This, I said, was about $65 a month.

"But wouldn't it be cheaper," he asked, "for the county to put everybody needing that kind of care into one or two large institutions?"

"Yes, if by cheap you mean what life means to us in terms of money only."

"But the tax-payers—wouldn't they be better satisfied?"

"I doubt it." And I told him I found people more and more concerned with the meaning of happiness to individuals; and that though individual tax-payers had complained to me about the cost of public assistance programs, these same tax-payers, interested in some one individual, insisted on the person's right to be provided for adequately.

"Why, yes," he said. "I'd hate to see old Mrs. B. sent to a large place like the County Poor Farm. It just wouldn't be right. I'll tell her about the Nursing Home." And then he added, with a chuckle, "I'm a tax-payer, but, you never can tell, I might be on relief myself, tomorrow."

The next conversation took place not in Cleveland but in New York.

[1] Conversation reported by Mrs. Lilah Anderson, caseworker, Cuyahoga County Relief Bureau, Cleveland.

Conversation with a Gag-Writer[1]

A friend of mine who is a gag-writer told me about an old man who asked him for the price of a cup of coffee. "I invited him into a diner to have the coffee with me," he said. "He told me he was on old age relief, and that he was getting only $15.90[2] a month for food. Could this be true?"

"Yes, if he was doing his own cooking." And I explained that the allowance had been worked out by dieticians as enough for a maintenance diet, "provided it was used wisely and with an eye to food values."

"Maybe a dietician could do it," he replied, "but this was a sick old man. . . . Why, it's only 50 cents a day! Does the city honestly expect anybody to live on such a niggardly bit? How can you stand working for such an outfit?"

I agreed the allowance was too small and then I explained that a public agency just carries out the will of the people, of whom he was one. . . . I asked if he had ever heard people grumble about taxes. Or if he had heard anyone say we shouldn't have relief now that everybody can get a job.

"Anyone!" he exclaimed, "I've even talked that way myself! And wisecracked about it on the radio!"

In the two above instances the opinions, fairly superficial at the outset, shifted easily. The following conversation shows a feeling against social workers which was perhaps deeper, and certainly more violent.

Conversation on a Train[3]

A naval officer on a train, a stranger, opened the conversation, "So you're a social worker, eh?" I said yes and

[1] Reported by Elizabeth R. Russell, case supervisor, New York City Department of Welfare.

[2] The standard amount of the grant at the time.

[3] Reported by Caroline A. Hughes, assistant supervisor of Social Service, Board of Children's Guardians, Trenton, New Jersey.

asked how he had known. He indicated the book I was reading, and added that he had taught psychology before the war. "But it was all the bunk. Psychology and all that stuff aren't what the boys out there need."

I said he must be in a good position to know about their needs and asked what he thought might be done for them that wasn't already being done. There must be a lot of things in spite of the concentrated efforts of all concerned.

"Do you mean social work? Social work isn't what's needed. The Red Cross is no damn good. All talk and procedures. No action. When a fellow really needs attention, I'd bet on the Salvation Army every time. There's an outfit with no fuss and feathers, that doesn't stop to ask a fellow if and what he needs. They can see that he does, and they hand out whatever is necessary for his comfort."

I said I was learning a lot. But that I had always found both the Red Cross and the Salvation Army most willing to co-operate to meet people's needs.

"Now what need would *you* ever have of either agency's help?"

I said social workers worked together to meet the many problems of those who needed us, regardless of the agency we worked for. I explained how necessary this was, for no one agency could meet every type of need.

He began to show some interest and asked what agency I worked for. I told him it was a public agency, and how many families and children we had under care.

He said, "It's all right to look out for the kids. But families could take care of themselves if someone just gave them enough money. They need decent living quarters and some recreation and jobs and that's all."

I agreed that they did need all these things, that often the chief trouble was financial, and that some families seemed to go along very well with financial aid alone. Then I said that as he probably knew, social workers as a body

64

were working toward legislation and other measures to bring about better living; for example, housing projects.

"O.K. But why do so many social workers stick their noses into people's private affairs?"

I said, "You'd be surprised how many people, rich or poor, need to talk over their problems with someone, and how many seek out our guidance and advice. Many people are not 'rich in friends,' and social workers often fill that need."

"What about those who don't want your advice?—those who just ask for cash?"

I explained why we had to ask questions, in order to establish eligibility, etc. Beyond that, I told him we tried to be careful about offering advice, unless it was asked. I said too that suggestions were different from commands which of course he, as a naval officer, knew!

He smiled. Then, a bit more interested, he said it must be quite a responsibility caring for so many children. "Does your agency have a lot of red tape? How long, for instance, do you keep people waiting before you decide to help them?"

I explained that social work had gone a long way in that respect, and how now we could grant emergency assistance before an investigation had been completed.

He said, "That's the way it should be done always."

I said, "In an emergency, yes. But we have the public to satisfy too. They furnish the funds and we owe them something, also."

Thinking that was enough about social work, I asked him if he had had leave for the holidays. He said he had been home to see his wife. He hung his head and said it had been very quiet at home. Then he told me his son had been killed a year ago. "That's why I joined up." Suddenly he was speaking about his son and of all the good times they used to have together.

He talked on and on, and I listened until the train pulled into my station. Then he said he guessed he'd talked too much to me about his troubles. He wanted to contribute something to "this fight" so that some of the other boys could come back home anyway.

I wished him luck. And then I said I hoped he wouldn't think too unkindly of social workers, because no matter what their agency, they were all working for the same things he was fighting for. He said, "Oh, they're really not so bad, but when I feel down, I have to pick on someone."

The caseworker's comment on this conversation is as revealing as the conversation itself:

I found it hard to talk to this man, because he was a stranger, was antagonistic, was attacking my profession, and used pretty rough language (which I have omitted) for more than half of the conversation. I knew I had to keep calm and not act defensive. I found it difficult to pick out the things about my work that might interest him and at the same time influence his attitude favorably toward social work. I felt overwhelmed by the challenge of interpretation to one who represented so many others who were probably bitter also. I was also somewhat daunted by his need for social work himself; and his violent opposition to social workers.

I was blocked not so much by any actual questions as by his over-all attitude. It was difficult to "stick with this" when he swore so much and so bitterly. However, after I learned why he was so bitter, I was glad I had kept at this job of interpretation.

I would have done better perhaps to have kept quiet longer or until I knew more of why he had taken such a dislike to social workers. For my own comfort I should not have let this seem the threat it did. Challenge is healthy; but a feeling of threat is not, when there's a job to be done!

The caseworker in the above conversation did not learn whether the naval officer had himself had an unhappy or baffling experience with a particular social agency. But countless social workers could report the difficulties of coping with the angers or scorn of persons who have had such experiences. Yet this is frequently accomplished. Take, for instance, the following report of a telephone call to the Child Welfare League of America on one of the touchiest subjects with which social workers must deal—the resentment of a person thwarted in his wish to adopt a child.

Conversation on the Telephone[1]

"Will you tell me," began an angry male voice, "what's the matter with your social agencies? Here we're offering our home, and a darn good one, and we can't get a baby! What's gumming up the works? Aren't there thousands of homeless children in institutions? Why can't we get at them?"

It's hard to give information to an angry man in any circumstances, and especially on the telephone. But I tried.

"Yes, you are right," I ventured, "there are thousands of children in institutions. But nearly all of them—over 95 per cent—have at least one parent, and many have both. They're not free for adoption. They're in institutions only until their own families can take care of them again."

"Hmm." He paused, but not for long. "But that other five per cent—why can't we get one of those babies?"

"Well, most of them aren't *babies*. Most of them are school age children—say six to sixteen."

"But we want a *baby*."

"I understand. That's how most people feel. And I hope you will be able to get one. But, do you know that nearly

[1] Reported by Mrs. Henrietta L. Gordon, information and publications secretary, Child Welfare League of America.

eight times as many people want to adopt babies as there are babies for adoption?"

"Really? But I thought—why, people used to be *urged* to adopt babies!"

"Yes. But that was back in the days when, if parents couldn't take good care of a child, there was nothing to do but take the child away and let it be adopted."

"Well, isn't that good sense?"

"No, because often the parents are only *temporarily* unable to take care of their child, and because a child really needs his own family. So if it's humanly possible, parents are helped to overcome whatever difficulty it is that keeps them from taking good care of their own children. Meanwhile, the social agency finds a good *temporary* place for a child, and does everything possible to strengthen his home ties, and to rehabilitate his home for him."

"Oh." He sounded less angry now.

"Another thing," I continued. "It used to be that a widow left with no income might have to give up her children, even though she loved them dearly and was a good mother. Now most states—including yours—provide a mother's assistance fund, so that these children can keep their own mother."

"Well, that does seem only right. We wouldn't want to take a child away from its mother. But what about children whose mothers die?"

"Not so many mothers die as used to. Many of the diseases which used to make orphans of children—tuberculosis, typhoid, smallpox, and illnesses and accidents in childbirth—have been curbed by the advances in medicine and hygiene. So you see, having fewer children for adoption really means we're becoming more civilized."

"Well, I suppose that's right," he conceded.

"Of course I know this doesn't help you directly, and I do hope the children's service agency in your city will be able to find a baby for you. But you might like to know, too, that the medical profession is finding that many childless couples can be helped to have children of their own. More than half of those who thought they couldn't have children, *can* have them. This means that those who can't will have a better chance of getting a child to adopt."

He considered this a moment. "Well," he concluded, "looks as if our chances are still pretty slim, with a social work outfit. Some people get babies in other ways—through doctors, or lawyers, don't they? And they get them, I hear, just as soon as they are born, instead of waiting several months."

"True, but they take a risk."

"Risk?"

"Yes. You see social agencies try to make adoption safe not only for the babies but for those who adopt them."

"What do you mean, safe for those who adopt them?"

"You can't always tell, till a baby is several months old, whether it is feeble-minded, for instance; or whether it was born with a physical disease or serious defect which doesn't show up and can't be tested for in a child's earliest weeks. And even aside from that, the adoption agency needs time to know a baby well enough to know the kind of home it needs, and to know the adopting parents well enough to know the kind of baby they want."

"Oh." And then, after a pause, "Why didn't someone tell me these things before? It's easier to take when you know the reasons."

This conversation, while it would not transmute a hatred for social agencies or social workers into enthusiasm, did give the angry man the information he needed to understand his experience. And this shifted his anger to a *why-wasn't-I-told* vexation, to which apparently he had every right. The conversation succeeded not only because it provided the facts, but because it gave them simply, without argument or apology, and upon the assumption that the man would be glad to know that these days there were fewer babies needing adoption. At the same time he could feel from the beginning that the social worker appreciated his wish to adopt one.

In all the above conversations the caseworkers had time to tell their story; or, if time was a factor, the interlocutors had come with direct queries to which needed information could be briefly given.

Sometimes there is no such leeway. This happens frequently in social contacts, where the question "Just what do you do?" is less a search for enlightenment than a gambit for getting acquainted or obliterating a silence. The caseworker then may have a chance only for a few brief words. Take the following conversation.

PARTY PATTER[1]

"A social worker?" The Viennese connoisseur of medieval art raised his eyebrows. "One of those psychiatric probers who hold people's hands and uncover their neuroses?"

I laughed, and said that I was indeed involved with neuroses, and that I had some fascinating clients.

He placed his fingers together in a peak and said, "If I had a great fortune to devote to philanthropy I would dedicate it to a foundation for the preservation of the neurosis." Social workers and psychiatrists, he continued, were always trying to remake people, with a general result of destroying their charm, and compelling them to analyze every situation so as to take all the spontaneity and pleasure out of it. "People are happier and more productive

[1] Reported by Ernestine Grindal, caseworker, Community Service Society of New York.

with their neuroses," he claimed, "and should be allowed to keep them!"

I told him that we were not concerned with those people who are happy with their neuroses, and that I would not tamper with his! Then I explained seriously that my professional problems involved people whose neurotic characteristics harmed other persons, their children, for instance; or themselves if they are unable to live acceptable lives within our present cultural setting. "A patient, for instance, who has not been able to leave her home in seven years, whose little boy has suffered accordingly, and whose husband, now in the Navy—and liking it—has been pressed to apply for a discharge because she couldn't manage without him." I dramatized my weekly difficulties in getting this woman to a hospital clinic. Fortunately, I could add that since she has begun to uproot her neuroses *my* days are more comfortable, as well as her own, her son's, and her husband's.

There wasn't time for more, and the caseworker felt she had hardly dented her acquaintance's predilection for the neurosis. Another conversation during that same evening also depressed her, though she felt she had cleared up a businessman's notions about the visionary, revolutionary and impractical nature of social workers, by explaining her agency's home economics department. By the time a third man asked her what she did, she replied flatly without enthusiasm, "I'm a social worker" and was ready to let it go at that.

"Oh, don't say it in that tone of voice!" he rebuked her, and asked specific questions about her agency and her caseload. He happened to be a board member of a family agency and the president of a settlement, and was himself enthusiastic about casework.

71

Many of the caseworkers who took part in the various experiments with conversation found in them a value beyond that of increasing their skill as interpreters. "They made me examine the *quality* of my casework," said one. "I discovered," said another, "that I tended to use the same case story over and over. I began to wonder if it was because that particular story was effective; or because I was lazy; or if it was because I didn't really have a good enough supply of cases in which I had really accomplished something to draw upon; and if not, why not."

Two or three caseworkers, whose duties included making occasional speeches to parent-teacher or other groups, reported that their experiments with conversations had helped their general "audience sense," providing a sort of guide and testing ground for material they could later use in speeches.

As we said in the previous chapter, the individual caseworker is expected to be able to tell about her work effectively and accurately. She gets little, if any, training—either in the course of her education or on the job—to help her meet this responsibility. Sometimes she meets it effectively, more often flounderingly. But by taking thought, by experiment, by self-scrutiny and conference-study, she can learn to do it much better. And she needs something beyond the basis of her own individual experience. She needs a wider knowledge of and a deeper confidence in the whole field of casework. She needs a clear-cut concept of her job. And she needs the backing of agency and interagency responsibility and action in the task of establishing good public relations.

CHAPTER IV

SEARCH FOR A COMMON DENOMINATOR

WE HAVE seen how, of all the questions which perplex caseworkers when asked what they do, *"Just what is casework?"* gives by far the most trouble. Not only the caseworker, but nearly everyone in a casework agency, from student-in-training to executive, from volunteer to president of the board, wishes for some simple statement which would convey accurate current knowledge of a changing service to a public with changing interests and needs.

Many social work writers have formulated definitions of casework. These range from authors of authoritative books on casework, and statisticians who try to measure casework in a given community or in a number of communities, to publicity specialists who prepare annual reports or leaflets for a single agency. No one of these definitions could satisfy the whole field or even a large part of it, any more than a definition of medicine could successfully convey the wide range from simple medication to psychotherapy. Casework, growing up in different settings, has reached different stages of development, has met differing needs, has operated under different auspices, and even under different philosophies. In a small town with only one social agency, a caseworker's function differs, perforce, from that of a caseworker in a city like Cleveland, where the community's supply of social agencies makes a more specialized job both possible and desirable.

Again, though many basic principles and techniques are common to all social casework—that, say, of the family agency, the child placement and adoption agency, the public welfare agency, the probation service of a court—the different structure of these agencies, the different specifications, legal and other, under which they must function, make it impossible to prepare an acceptable over-all definition. More rewarding is a search for the common denominators.

Unlike medicine and law—about which a general if vague public knowledge exists, and where lack of more specific knowledge does not so greatly hobble the usefulness of these professions—the field of casework, as we have said, feels the need, if not of definition, at least of some current definitive or descriptive statement. The caseworker wishes some such formulation partly for clarity's sake; partly as a resource to use when telling an unknowing public—or even some of the slightly acquainted publics—what she does.

To work toward some such statement, the Cleveland Advisory Committee to our study of casework interpretation appointed two subcommittees.

The first, made up of caseworkers[1] from various fields, undertook to set down the concept of casework which they wished people to know and understand. The second subcommittee, made up of writers—both

---

[1] This committee consisted of the chairman, Mrs. Rae Carp Weil, Jewish Family Service Association; Mrs. Prudence Kwiecien, Youth Bureau; Mrs. James K. Macdougall and Mrs. Sidney J. Berkowitz, both of Family Service Association; and Mrs. Elsie Martens Waelder, then associate professor of casework of the faculty of the School of Applied Social Sciences, Western Reserve University.

newspaper reporters and public relations personnel[1]—
would then examine the caseworkers' statement from
the angle of public interest and recast it lucidly for a
general public.

These assignments, which at first glance seemed
simple, required an unexpected amount of time and
thought from both groups. The caseworkers met some
half dozen times to discuss what they should include.
Next they prepared two preliminary drafts and sub-
mitted them to the general committee. Then, using
this committee's suggestions, they worked out a statement, ready to hand on to the writers' committee.

The writers' chief criticisms had to do not with
content but with phrasing and organization of material. One member thought the statement overquali-
fied; another that it was a series of abstractions;
another that it needed, if not specific case stories, at
least illustrative material. One summed up what
seemed to be the general opinion: that it was a good
statement of what casework was about, but that it
could be better written. "You could squeeze out two-
thirds of the verbiage in the first two paragraphs and
still get the same message across." And, "Even professional writing could be made Anglo-Saxon."

The writers' committee then decided that each of
its members should rewrite the statement, or write

[1] This committee consisted of the chairman, Raymond A. Bruner,
director of publicity for Western Reserve University; Anna B. Beattie,
educational secretary, Family Service Association; Mrs. Louise Bruner,
columnist and special writer for Cleveland News; Jack Yeaman Bryan,
then director of public relations, Welfare Federation of Cleveland; Marie
Daerr, Cleveland Press; Mrs. Helen Allyn MacDonald, Cleveland Press;
Janelle Moser, assistant, Publicity Department, Cleveland Community
Fund; and Todd Simon, Cleveland Plain Dealer.

another growing out of the discussion of it. Four of them did so.

When these separate statements had been considered by both committees, one writer made a final draft[1] which included all the ideas agreed upon. This was approved by the larger advisory committee. It has since been much used by individual agencies.

Because the process of working toward the final draft was found valuable to the caseworkers who took part in the experiment and may be useful to others, we present here the various statements out of which it evolved.

First we have arranged in parallel columns, the caseworkers' basic statement and one writer's restatement, with "some of the verbiage squeezed out."

THE CASEWORKERS' STATEMENT

Social casework has had as its objective through the years the highest development of family life in order that the individual members of the family may have opportunity to achieve personally satisfying and socially useful lives.

The quality of the life of any given community depends in large measure upon the quality of life of each family within that community. Out of the healthy family comes the individual who has experienced democratic living in his family

THE STATEMENT OF A WRITER[2]

Social casework aims to develop the life of a family so that its members can live useful, satisfying lives.

How a community lives depends largely on how its families live. Healthy family life teaches democratic living, sharing of opportunities and responsibilities, respect for others' rights and contributions, self-respect, tolerance, and joint

[1] See p. 89.

[2] By Todd Simon.

76

group. Here he first learns to share opportunities and responsibilities, privileges and duties; here he learns respect for the rights and contributions of others and for himself; and achieves tolerance of difference, and the use of capacities in co-operation with others for common happiness and social usefulness.

In normal family life there are inevitably ups and downs. Growth is not here solely a matter of upward, forward movement. The mere daily living together of a group of people with different personalities, ideas, and drives produces healthy differences of opinion, and sometimes sharp conflict and tense feelings. Through such experiences come growth, greater strength, and independence. However, if the too-sharp differences are not accepted, nor the conflicts solved relatively well, a situation may arise in which the individual energies may be paralyzed, or are expended treadmill fashion, and growth does not continue.

Again, there may be periods in which the conditions of the external world press in upon the family excessively. Such periods as those of economic depressions and world wars

useful work for joint happiness.

Ups and downs can't be avoided in normal family life. Growth is not always upward and forward. Just living with other people produces healthy disagreements, and sometimes sharp conflict and tense feelings. Such experiences breed growth, greater strength and independence. But growth stops if too-sharp differences are not accepted or worked out well. Then the individual's energies may be paralyzed, or spent going over and over the ground of conflict.

Outside pressures, too—like depressions or wars — force many and great changes in a family's life. This pressure may forge stronger families and stronger individuals, but it may involve numerous and great changes in the life of the family group. From those experiences may emerge a stronger family and stronger individuals, but for some families and individuals the demands may prove too great and normal development is delayed, stability is broken, and a downward trend may set in.

Social caseworkers have assumed responsibility for helping others when personal and family lives have become entangled, and when external difficulties have seemed to overpower the individual and family strength. In so helping, social workers have called upon already existing resources, the fields of medicine, psychiatry, education, law, and others. They have also, from their own experiences and practice in helping others, developed a body of knowledge and skills especially their own, casework skills which enable the individual to use his strength and abilities to solve personal and family difficulties, and to make the best of or improve external social difficulties.

Therefore, it is usually desirable that the social caseworker have, in addition to the accepted four years of undergraduate work, specialized training

also overwhelm some, delaying normal growth and breaking down their stability.

This is the point where social caseworkers offer help. They call in other trained helpers—doctors and nurses, psychiatrists, teachers, and lawyers. And they use their own special skills, which they learn while helping others, showing troubled people how to use their own strength and abilities to solve their personal and family problems.

To be a caseworker, one must like and understand people, and be able to inspire confidence in those needing help. That is why special studies in based upon this body of knowledge and experience in the understanding of human behavior. The caseworker must be a person who likes and understands people. She must be able to inspire confidence in those she is to help and be willing to help.

The way in which the caseworker helps a person deal with the ever-common problems of life varies with the nature of the difficulty and with the person's real wishes and abilities. Since each bit of help given must be appropriate to the particular problem of a particular person, it is inevitable that the method will be highly individualized.

Certain aspects of the casework method (or way of helping) are generally common to all situations, however. One of these is that the caseworker must understand how people feel when worried, upset, nervous. She must be able to comprehend the quality of fears, doubts, anger, or misgivings when uncontrolled and not understood, and how these feelings may prompt behavior which seems illogical or proves unfruitful. She must also be aware of the important facts of a particular difficulty, for mutual understanding of the

how people act, and why, and in what can be done about it, are usually added to the caseworker's four years of college work.

When people are worried, upset, nervous, or are angry, or afraid, or feel beaten, they often do things that make a bad situation worse. A caseworker must understand people's feelings under such stress. She must step in, learn what is causing the trouble, and then help the ones who want to find a better way to work out the problem, each case in its own way.

trouble, how the difficulty came about, and what it means to those concerned. She needs too to find out what changes the person seeking help would really like to bring about since her goal is to help him deal with his problem in his own way.

These things then are usual: that the caseworker knows psychology, learns the facts of a particular case, and helps the person do something about his situation himself.

The highly individualized part of the casework method comes in the specific way in which the caseworker learns the relevant facts about the difficulty and what she does when she knows them.

Sometimes the caseworker has knowledge of resources in the community which someone else, meeting a particular kind of problem for the first time, does not have. Perhaps all the help given is to tell the person where he can find a special school for his child, a home for an aged relative, medical service, better housing. Again, the caseworker may be able to give advice on a particular matter about which she has more knowledge than the person seeking help; or she can give financial assistance for support of the family, or assist in making

Some cases need only a word from the caseworker on where a child can get special schooling, where an aged relative can be given a home, how to get medical help.

Sometimes she can give advice out of her own experience and knowledge. She can help with money, or by lining up health or schooling opportunities.

80

available special health or educational opportunities when any one of these may be the chief thing needed to help get the family or individual back on an even keel.

Other times, the person who seeks casework help may be so close to his problem or so upset about it that he cannot see the woods for the trees. The caseworker can help him "walk around the woods," and see his problem from all angles. With this fresh viewpoint he is able to make a decision more wisely, based upon a more complete and cool-headed consideration of the total situation.

Other people who come to the caseworker may be standing in the way of their own happiness because they are feeling or acting in a way that does not fit the situation they are trying to meet. This often happens because we learn to act certain ways through experience and do not always stop acting in the old way when the experiences change and are new and different. We may get into a rut of thinking that things don't go well for us even when they begin to go well, or of thinking we are inferior and inexperienced after we have learned and know how to do something. The same thing may

People with problems often are too close to them to see them from all angles. Or they get into a rut in their thinking and feelings. They think they are failures, and expect to fail in each new test. They think they are not loved, when they really are.

81

be true of our feelings; we may feel that we are of no account when we are or could be, or that we are not loved when we really are. With people concerned with such trouble, the caseworker helps in two ways: first, to find out herself and help the person find out why he learned to act or feel in this way; then to help him to see what the present situation is so that he can discard the old, inappropriate way of acting and act more realistically in terms of what the present situation calls for.

Caseworkers find out how people got into those habits, show the people themselves how they got into them, and then help them see how they can be happier by changing their old ways of acting.

Everyone has periods in which things go wrong; it is not necessary for these periods to continue, for casework is a way of helping to get the difficulty straight. If casework help is sought before the problems become too severe or overwhelming, more effective help may be obtained, painful experiences may be avoided, and the ability to move forward independently will be strengthened.

Everyone has periods when things go wrong. The earlier a person in trouble asks for casework, the better his chance of getting his problems solved. Painful experiences can be avoided if he gets early casework help, and he can then move forward more and more surely on his own.

Some of the caseworkers who prepared the original statement found it of value to compare the two above versions, sentence by sentence. They agreed that the rewrite omitted no essential idea, and that its simpler style, and substitution of Anglo-Saxon for Latin-derived words, made it better not only for a general but for a professional audience. They found, too, that this briefer, clearer version showed them their faults in form and organization.

OTHER STATEMENTS

The author of the simplified statement also wrote an article to show how the same basic ideas could be used quite differently in an agency bulletin story. This version has special interest because of its concrete and pictorial writing.

The Tack in the Upholstery

Even before they break their first rattle, people have problems. They have all kinds of them as long as they live.

A bottle of warm milk will solve some early problems.

Bandages solve a lot of them a few years later, and pills, shots, play pens, orange juice and rest in bed solve some more.

Calm words and a few good, warm hugs solve some others. And later on, getting that outlandish windbreaker, bobby socks or the pork pie hat the other kids are wearing will solve the next ones.

Marriage solves some problems and brings a new set of them. It is the same way with having children, getting a divorce, moving to another neighborhood.

Some problems can be solved with a hammer. A tack works loose and sticks out through the upholstery. When you find it, you can get it out. Or you can tap it back in place.

But there are some troubles that don't work out that easily.

A man gets laid off. Job-hunting may get him over that one. If job-hunts don't do it, landlords and the washing machine payment and food bills can make that man's home a hell of worries and battles.

Even when war has not taken away the breadwinner—
even when unemployment has not ground a family's diet
down to beans and biscuit—there can be frictions, troubles
and pain. No family is safe from it just because they have
money or intelligence or education or even goodwill.

One child knows his sister is the favorite. That hurts.
A wife suspects her husband is in love with another woman.
A marriage totters because it started off wrong. Once man
and wife, now the couple is just a boarder and a housekeeper. Dirty dishes. Diapers and crying. Job troubles.
Auto accidents and bills. And fights, arguments, accusa-
tions, punishments, desertions, runaways, cold meals,
whisky, what not.

All the vitamins, money and hammers in the world cannot solve such problems. The tack in the upholstery digs
and tears. It rips your clothes. It scratches and stabs your
flesh. And you can't rest there and you can't find the tack.

A guy at the office says I'd get a divorce. Uncle Emil says
I'd sit down and give that woman a good talking to. The
school principal writes that this boy needs stricter home
discipline. The neighbors discuss it, and pump information
from the kids.

Before you can hit a thing, you have to find it. The tack
in the upholstery is hidden. Or it may have caught in your
clothing, and you can't see it because it is too near you,
although someone else might see it plain as day.

There are people fitted and trained to find tacks like
these, and to get them back in place. They are called caseworkers. The sooner they are called in on the case, the less
damage will be done.

Caseworkers think this way:

"Here we have all kinds of problems, each a little different. And here is a kit of tools to help solve them: doctors
and nurses and hospitals, teachers and schools of several
kinds; camps, scouting, settlement houses and foster
homes; homes for aged people, psychiatrists and clinics,

even money and clothing and special foods and budget experts.

"And then a special tool—the caseworker's own skill in helping troubled people to find the tack, the point of the problem, to look at it squarely, and then to find a good way to get rid of it."

Even in badly hurt, hopeless people there are strong, good impulses. After the problem is found and faced, those will be the foundation of a new pattern of action.

Caseworkers are people who like to help others understand themselves and their mates and their children. But just by being outside the family problem, third parties a little apart from the battleground, they are useful.

When we are ruffled, we will admit to this third party what we would never admit to the one we fought with. That would be giving in. That would be like quitting, taking the blame for the trouble.

Talking out troubles makes us feel better. But we would rather talk them out to someone who specializes in understanding, and who can then explain things and get us going on a new plan. It isn't just talking troubles out. If that were all we needed, we could dig a hole in the back yard and into it speak all our worries and woes. We need understanding, sympathy, respect, and help in getting snarled ideas and feelings combed out straight. Once sorted out, these ideas and feelings can be aimed in different and better directions.

It is a hard job growing up. Living with others can frighten, can thwart or even crush some of us. Caseworkers know that, and know something can be done to help the growing process. They know of no paradise. They know some pressures and jabs only make us grow stronger and more independent and richer and happier and more useful.

They also know some pin-point problems can rob us of rest, make us do wry and destructive things, make us cramped and unhappy. They find the subtle, digging, gnawing things that make us sick at heart, and they help us make ourselves get rid of the trouble so that we can be well again.

The above article presented by specific illustration the essence of the basic statement. The next two statements take a different slant.

The first of these, prepared by Louise Bruner and Raymond A. Bruner, answers the question "What is casework?" by highlighting the professional nature of casework and the qualifications of a good caseworker.

Casework

Definition of casework. Casework is a type of social service performed to improve the life and outlook of a family or an individual in distress.

Traditionally the work is done by a judge, businessman, doctor, lawyer, pastor, priest or rabbi, or any individual with judgment, stability, and common sense. Because of the complexity of modern life and the large amount of specialized knowledge accumulated to help persons in distress, casework has become a profession requiring special training. Much of the training is now done by schools of social work.

The distress which a caseworker seeks to alleviate may or may not be caused by lack of income or other means of livelihood. It may be due to mental or emotional disturbance, conflict, inability to get along with others, family quarrels, and similar causes.

Duties and qualifications of a caseworker. The professionally trained caseworker has a sound working knowledge of sociology and psychology, a general understanding of modern medical science, and a knowledge of public and private agencies set up to deal with human problems. The caseworker, before receiving specialized training, is expected to have a good mentality, sound judgment, common sense, emotional stability and some degree of liberal education.

The professional worker treats each case as a separate entity, the individual as well as the disease. The worker is expected to have a good enough personality to inspire the confidence of those under treatment, and to observe a strict code of ethics to deal fairly without prejudice and without betraying confidences.

After the above paragraphs the authors, to show that "casework goes beneath surface manifestations," round out their article with three briefly stated examples of casework service—one to a child, one to a serviceman's wife, and one to an old couple.

The next writer, Jack Yeaman Bryan, also discusses casework as a profession. He, too, tells the story anew, presenting not case stories but rather specific questions which come to the caseworker. He restates simply and effectively the basic assumptions and principles of casework.

What IS Casework?

Casework is a profession devoted to helping individuals with personal and family problems. It is concerned in particular with emotional or practical difficulties which endanger a person's stability and happiness.

How can I make my child's behavior more agreeable? Shall I seek a divorce or is there some way to work out a satisfactory married life? My expenses are running ahead of my income—how can I make ends meet? My mother, recently widowed, is chronically ill, but we have no room for her in our apartment—how can I arrange for her care? These are a few of the many problems which caseworkers are trained to deal with.

No matter what the problem may be, casework seeks, first of all, to understand all the facts of the situation so as to help the affected person solve it in his own way. Casework takes care not to encourage or increase dependence. On the contrary, it helps its clients find ways of becoming free of paralyzing or insurmountable difficulties so as to achieve a new independence.

To do this it is essential to make a careful and sympathetic study of each client's situation. That, in fact, is the principal reason why the profession is known as *casework;* that is, it always deals with individual cases. Furthermore, since the circumstances in any case may be peculiar, the caseworker does not use prefabricated solutions. The way of dealing with the circumstances may vary considerably with each case, and every step of service is adjusted to the needs peculiar to the client and his family. These, too, constitute additional reasons for the name *casework.*

Casework is concerned, most of all, about problems that affect family well-being. It works on the assumption that healthy, happy family life is a basic source of strength for our national life. Any problem which disrupts the harmony or welfare of the family affects the general welfare and represents the kind of problem caseworkers are especially trained to handle. Casework training, in other words, is primarily designed for providing service that will strengthen family life.

For a very large range of family problems, the caseworker can give all the service necessary. Many family problems, of course, may also require the help of other experts—perhaps a physician, an attorney, a psychiatrist, a banker, or an employment counselor. If so, the caseworker is equipped to tell just where the right kind of service can be found.

One of the principles most carefully adhered to is that all information which a client gives a caseworker is kept in strict confidence. This makes it possible for a person to

SEARCH FOR A COMMON DENOMINATOR

talk over intimate family problems with a caseworker, remaining sure that the information will be used only in ways of benefit to himself.

At the final joint meeting of the writers' and caseworkers' subcommittees, the above papers were compared and discussed. Everyone was struck with the variety with which the material was treated; with the fact that no two persons used it the same way. But the committee wanted a final manuscript which would include all the ideas of the writers and the caseworkers. One of the writers, Todd Simon, volunteered to put them together. Here is the final synthesized statement.

Casework—What Is It?

Casework is a profession which helps a troubled person to find what is causing his personal or family problems, and to see what he can do to solve them.

Caseworkers are trained for this service of discovering the broad range of human ills and of helping each individual to decide what remedies among those available would be best for him.

Healthy people have pains and worries, and they get over them. So do healthy families. A child gets measles and then gets well. Couples have spats and then make up. Daughters use lipstick too soon, and sons beg for the family car and keep it out too late. We solve these problems and grow on them. Sometimes we can stand even the massive pain of a crippling accident, of war, and unemployment and still not break.

But sometimes these pressures can overwhelm us. Homes can become so tense that the strain throws out trouble warnings. A child sleeps in school, or he ducks out the door as his father comes up the front steps. Nagging turns to shrill quarreling. Parents fight over taking in grandparents.

Troubled people worry. They don't know what to do. They lie awake going over their problem while the wires that link up the family pull taut and seem ready to snap.

This is where a caseworker can help. No one should go into casework unless she likes people and enjoys helping them win their way out of trouble toward a happier life. To get her job she has had to go through college and then take special training, usually in a school of social science. She studies psychology, the family, and society.

Such a school, and the agencies that hire caseworkers, expect her to be intelligent, unprejudiced, and well balanced, and to have good judgment, common sense, and understanding.

She learns how to deal sympathetically with the upset, unhappy ones who will come to her for help. She learns how to look below the surface for the root of trouble. She learns what tools are at hand to treat the wide array of problems she must meet. There are eye problems, and there are sight-saving classes in schools. Chronic illness can be met with nursing. For aged relatives needing special care there may be rest homes. She learns to spot problems and to know community resources and to pick the satisfactory clinic or social agency which can best serve each individual case.

Also, she works with the personalities in the upset home. Her job is first to understand what is troubling the individual. Then she helps this vexed person himself to understand his problem. She helps him find inside himself, inside the home, or in health and welfare agencies the resources to rebuild his family's life. With her help, he chooses those changes he can make in his actions, in his home situation, or his work, that promise to make him and his family happier.

A man may try to dominate his children and find they are getting into one bad scrape after another. He may come to decide he must change his way with them. In himself, with help, he may find enough love for those youngsters to outweigh his pride and his old habits of shouting them into obedience. In even hopeless, beaten people are such stores of love, tolerance or ability to sacrifice—as when parents must agree to place a child in a foster home to help solve the child's problem and theirs.

Caseworkers set out these discovered inner resources before their clients just as they put before them outside resources like psychiatrists, legal help, or nurseries or camping chances. They inspire them with confidence enough to face their home realities and to go back willing to change them. That builds the independence needed to take the onset of new daily problems, to solve them by sharing loads and rewards in a home pleasant with mutual respect.

All this is done in friendliness. It is never forced upon people. The client is assured his confidences are safe with someone who wants to help, both for the job of solving a problem and because a good solution will add to the community's order and richness. Casework's help aims to bring the trouble down so that families can take up again that healthy home life which is the small image of our nation's democratic way, and a main source of its strength.

This statement was presented to the general Advisory Committee, which accepted it with enthusiasm. It was regarded not as an all-purpose description of casework to end all descriptions, but rather as a basic statement which individual agencies could adapt and change, add to and subtract from, and combine with their own material according to need, and illustrate with facts, figures, and examples.

Cleveland's casework agencies have already put it to wide use. It has provided information and stimulus to staffs, both professional and clerical; to boards; to committees, especially public relations committees; to Big Sister and Big Brother groups, and Junior League groups, and to other volunteers. Some 200 copies were sent to the public librarian in charge of public school libraries, to be included with other material for the use of teachers in the Community Fund campaign. It was also used in agency bulletins, sent to a mailing list of several thousand.

In most of these instances the statement was used not as a thing in itself but as one part of wider effort of imparting information.

One of the highest values of an experiment such as this search by caseworkers and writers for a sound, simple, descriptive statement about casework,[1] is the stimulus it provides for further search and research. The statement achieved by the Committee makes it easier but no less important for each agency and for groups of agencies to continue to work out new descriptive material. Because of the developing nature of casework and the ever-changing and widening scene in which it must be practiced, there will always be a need to scrutinize past descriptions and to develop new ones.

---

[1] An interesting by-product of this experiment was the effect it had upon one of the newspapermen. He said it had taught him a good deal; that he had, of course, known about casework but "it wasn't until I had to verbalize it that I really took it all in."

CHAPTER V

PUBLIC ATTITUDES TOWARD CASEWORK

SOCIAL caseworkers count on little understanding of casework from the general public. They tend to look for only limited acceptance and much adverse feeling, ranging from vague distaste to antagonism. On what are these timid expectations based?

There is, of course, no such thing as public opinion about casework in the sense that there is public opinion about disarmament or world government. Many small, separate publics, whose nuclei are the people who use or support casework, do know and have opinions about it. A much larger public, potential in relation to casework, is actual so far as the broader concepts of *social work* are concerned—the public made up of millions of persons who contribute to community chests. Beyond these, there is the so-called general public, little informed about modern social work, yet a partner with it in the acceptance and carrying out—though often grudgingly—of many of its aims: the public whose elected representatives, for instance, vote relief and various social security measures into law; and which supports them by taxes.

The individual members of these publics hold conflicting views about social work, or measures sponsored by social workers. Their opinions grow out of what they have experienced, or observed, or have been told; or how they feel some particular measure will affect them personally—what it will cost them, or how it will benefit them.

These cross currents of thought and feeling show themselves variously: In the enactment into laws of many measures sponsored by social work; and the frequent failures of such laws to provide for the trained personnel essential to carry out the public intent. In increasing demands upon private social agencies and their failure to recruit sufficient personnel. In the refusal of many veterans—and others—to heed the referrals of information centers to casework agencies; and their increasing willingness to use such agencies if they can pay for the services, or if there is no tag of "welfare" or "charity" in the agency titles. In the continued confusion of charity and social work, and the old angers against charity. In the persisting clichés—such as "How much of our money really goes to those in need?" and in the sneering epithets such as "do-gooder" or "uplifter" which survive in the public vocabulary. In the increased support of social work, and its spread to new fields. In the growing number of students trying to get into schools of social work. In the comparatively low salaries of social workers.

But all such a list tells us is that people feel differently about social work. Which feelings prevail? How much farther than it now goes would the public, the various publics, be willing to go in the provision of the various social work services, if they knew about them? What do the people of any community really know and how do they think and feel about social work, and specifically about casework?

94

THE CLEVELAND PUBLIC OPINION POLL

Various communities or agencies in communities have tried to find some of the answers. One such effort was the Cleveland poll, made in the spring of 1945 under the auspices of the School of Applied Social Sciences of Western Reserve University.[1]

This poll grew out of a suggestion from one of the newspaper members of the Advisory Committee for our present study, but was not made as part of this study; only about half of its wide range of questions — which included various health, welfare, and economic subjects—had to do with opinions about casework.

The poll covered a fairly large sampling, however, including in all some 700 women, interviewed by 28 students in Western Reserve's School of Applied Social Sciences. All these students had had some training in interviewing, and some had worked on polls before. Mrs. B. J. Purvis, an instructor of interviewers for the National Public Opinion Survey (the Roper Poll) helped prepare them for this particular

[1] Overmyer, Richard P., Here's the Score in Cleveland. Department of Public Relations, Welfare Federation of Cleveland, 1945 (mimeographed). "The poll originated in a group of social workers, newspaper men and public relations people who had been called together to act as advisers in a research project for the Russell Sage Foundation. It was conducted in the most scientific manner, using the methods of probably the most reliable nation-wide polling organization, and its results were analyzed carefully by a committee of experts before they were publicized. Suggestion of the poll came from Todd Simon, reporter for Cleveland Plain Dealer. The committee of analysts was headed by Dr. R. Clyde White, professor of public welfare in the School of Applied Social Sciences at Western Reserve University, and included W. Thomas McCullough, research secretary of the Welfare Federation, and Henry L. Zucker, then secretary of the Federation's Casework and Children's Councils. Jack Bryan, then director of public relations for the Welfare Federation, supervised and coordinated the entire project."

poll. The findings were tabulated by a trained research analyst, Mrs. Brooks W. MacCracken.

Nine of the 18 questions included in the questionnaire used in this poll brought out material bearing directly or indirectly on the subject of our study. These nine are given below.[1] Although the term "social worker" and not "caseworker" is used, the questions suggest the kinds of personal service which caseworkers give:

1. In an institution where children are cared for, how important do you think it is to have someone present to study the personal problems of each child, keep in touch with his home, and assist him in making a good adjustment? Very important. Important. Not so Important. Don't Know.

2. Do you think social work is (a) for poor people only, or (b) for all sorts of people, including those who can pay for service?

3. Under what conditions would *you* seek help from a social worker?

4. Suppose you know a couple whose quarreling is so serious that it is affecting their children. Where do you think they could get help? (Number according to order of choice.)

a. Doctor
b. Lawyer
c. Newspaper columnist
d. Policeman
e. Social worker
f. Political leader or councilman
g. Court
h. Pastor
i. Psychiatrist
j. Mr. Anthony
k. Welfare Federation
l. Other
m. Don't know

Reason for first choice:

[1] The numbering here does not follow that in the questionnaire which is reproduced in Appendix A, p. 227.

5. Suppose you were the parent of a 14-year-old boy or girl who was running wild and getting out of your control. From which of the following would you seek help? (Number according to order of choice):

a. Juvenile court
b. Newspaper columnist
c. Institute of Family
   Service
d. Settlement house
e. Mr. Anthony
f. School principal
g. Youth Bureau
h. Girl Scouts or
   Boy Scouts
i. Pastor

j. Social worker
k. Policeman
l. Welfare Federation
m. Political leader or
   councilman
n. Cleveland Guidance
   Center
o. YMCA or YWCA
p. Other
q. Don't know

6. If a serviceman's wife is having trouble with her family affairs, where do you think she should go for help?

7. Suppose you know an unmarried girl who is going to have a baby. Where, outside her family, would you suggest that she go for help?

8. Suppose you had a serious personal or family problem. To whom would you go for help?

9. Would you mind telling me your idea of a social worker?

The poll aimed not only to uncover public attitudes, but perhaps especially to be in itself a public relations enterprise. The Cleveland newspapers widely publicized its findings—especially the Plain Dealer, which ran a series of articles under the by-line of Todd Simon, the reporter who suggested the poll. We shall quote at some length from these articles, partly because the way in which the poll information reached the public is pertinent to our study of the public relations of casework; and partly because of the reporter's skill in fusing the statistical findings, their interpretation, and interviews with specialists.

Before the poll was taken, the last question, "Would you mind telling me your idea of a social worker?" was thought by some to be apologetic and weighted with the expectation of unfavorable replies. Some others thought it might lead in the opposite direction, tending to make people soften the expression of any disapproval they might feel. It may have had both of these effects, or neither.

A preliminary survey of 50 persons either connected with or familiar with social work showed that they looked for a large measure of adverse comment. "Many agency executives and board members estimated that 30, 40, or 50 per cent of the people polled would have unfavorable ideas about social workers."[1]

Yet only 3 per cent of the 700 women questioned in the poll regarded social workers unfavorably.

The Plain Dealer's reporter, under the headline "Social Workers Win Poll Plaudits," discussed both the expectations and the answers to this question:

The results should wipe away social workers' inferiority complexes in one sweeping squee-gee action.

Every social work executive and leader of public opinion asked to estimate what percentage of the answers would be unfavorable was caught away off base—except three persons.

Nearest estimates were those of Paul Bellamy, editor of the Plain Dealer, who said five per cent would be unfavor-

[1] Overmyer, Richard P., Here's the Score in Cleveland.

able, Mrs. William C. Treuhaft, chairman of the Federation group work council, who guessed five per cent, and James E. Ewers, director of the County Child Welfare Board, who guessed ten.

Actually, only three per cent of the answers were definitely unfavorable. An additional six per cent had some unfavorable tone mixed into the response. Thirty per cent were outright favorable reactions, 46 per cent just neutral descriptions without praise or blame and the rest were no-answer or don't know replies.[1]

These were typical women of all economic levels, saying to poll takers: "Trained people who have an aptitude for helping others." . . . "Generally they are cold-blooded. They haven't enough of the milk of human kindness." . . . "Interested in people and their problems. I don't know any, but they visit homes, suggest nursing and the kinds of food people should prepare." . . . "A condescending, superior, well-educated person who is not quite human and who tells you how to dispose of your life." . . . "Grand people. Should have a good personality. Should be willing to help people and try to understand them." . . . "Women who look after children who are not cared for." . . . "To me she is a sort of big sister to the community. The

[1] The Welfare Federation report on Here's the Score in Cleveland analyzes these comments in further detail: "Of those who gave well informed descriptions of the activities of social workers, 43 were favorable, 88 were neutral, three were unfavorable, and two gave mixed reactions. Of those who gave incomplete or vague descriptions of activities, 96 were favorable, 164 neutral, nine unfavorable, and 22 mixed. Of those who described personal characteristics only, 70 were favorable, 63 neutral, 15 unfavorable, and 21 mixed. The sum of all this is that only three per cent of those who answered the question actually had unfavorable opinions about social workers. There was a great and encouraging variety of comments in the answers to this question which should be very heartening to all people in the social work field. One or two said, 'have easy jobs and big salaries,' but the following are more typical: 'Does a grand job for not half enough pay—must get a lot of satisfaction out of what they are doing'; 'very fine—human and younger than they used to be—they have better understanding of people.'"

average one is someone you could go to and talk over your troubles and problems."

Harry F. Affelder, [then] Welfare Federation president, had guessed 30 per cent of the replies would be unfavorable to social workers—just ten times more than really were. "We were astonished and delighted by this evidence of an extremely small negative feeling toward social work," he said yesterday. "Social work has evidently proved its worth in a way which is convincing to a very large majority of Greater Clevelanders."

Asked why he put his guess as low as five per cent, Bellamy explained: "Most of us know very well that social work is doing a lot of good here, and we are ready to back it. I don't see what would make more than five people in every 100 find any serious fault with it."

The editor of the News, N. R. Howard, estimated 30 per cent of replies would be unfavorable. Louis B. Seltzer, Press editor [now president of the Welfare Federation], judged that 50 per cent would be unfavorable.

Mrs. Treuhaft, who shared honors with Bellamy for the closest guess, said one in four of social agency board members and trustees would say that social workers were idealistic, impractical or radical. "But the majority of people have a different view because so many of the general population have received some help from social workers," she added. "They know social workers by what is done in their own homes, not by what is said in meetings."

"Sixty-eight per cent—more than two in every three— of Cleveland families have at one time or another received social work service," said W. T. McCullough, Welfare Federation research secretary. He said this was learned through clearings of names of draftees. "Scouting and Y. W. and Y. M. C. A. services would increase this percentage," he said. "The 68 per cent were those given some sort of personal service such as that given by family service or child care or health agencies."

Another poll question, which bore specifically upon the use of casework in children's institutions, brought preponderantly favorable answers.

Under the headline "Case Work Gets Vote of Women," and a subhead "Poll Shows 80% Consider It 'Very Important,'" the Plain Dealer's reporter writes:

Once they know what it does, Greater Cleveland women fully approve of that foggy-sounding profession called "casework."

Poll-takers who sampled public opinion for the Welfare Federation asked the women this question: "How important do you think it is for an institution where children are cared for to have someone on duty who would study the personal problems of each child, keep in touch with his home and assist him in making a good adjustment?"

Eighty per cent answered: "Very important." Another 15 per cent said: "Important." Only two per cent said: "Not so important," and three per cent did not know.

"If we had asked them how important it is to have a caseworker in such institutions," said Dr. R. Clyde White, chief poll analyst, "very few would have known what we were talking about."

Cleveland had only one child-caring institution giving casework service to its boys and girls in 1930. There are now 16 child institutions which do casework. Savings in money, spreading of service to more children and quicker replacement of the child in its own home are brought by casework, according to a study at Bellefaire, one of the Community Fund children's homes.

"We started offering casework in 1940," said Leon H. Richman, Bellefaire's executive director. "Children stayed at Bellefaire an average of six years and two months then. Each year, with caseworkers bringing every community resource to bear on the problem, preparing both child and relatives for the return home, we have reduced the average stay. It came down to two years and seven months in 1944, and in the first six months of 1945 it has come down to two years and two months. That is a total cut of nearly two-thirds. The saving to the community is obvious."

Similar gains in Community Fund institutions caring for Catholic children were indicated by Rev. A. J. Murphy, director of the Catholic Charities Bureau. "We always used to have overlong stays," he said. "Our institutions were always clogged up and the facilities had to be closed to large numbers of children who also needed care. Now there is a more constant flow in and out because case-workers help children become prepared more rapidly to return to their homes. The caseworker has become the golden strand binding the child to his family, and vice versa. The caseworker not only handles the child's own personal problems with delicacy and understanding, but also helps the parents to get back on an even keel so they can repair the home situation and let the child come back under more wholesome circumstances.

"The child is no longer on a tiny, isolated island, cut off from the rest of the community, when in an institution. Instead, all the advantages within the community are now used to restore him to normal home life."

Alfred S. Winters, director of the Children's Aid Society, a child study home, said: "Home situations are often the real source of a child's difficulty. Unless the home's troubles are solved while the child is cared for some place else, the result can't be more than 50 per cent effective. You can't cure an infection until you heal its source, and you can't correct a behavior problem until you remove its cause."

Some of the questions tested both opinion and knowledge about social work. One of these was, "Do you think social work is (a) for poor people only, or

(b) for all sorts of people, including those who can pay for the service?"

In view of the frequently held idea that social work and the meeting of material needs are the same, the replies to this question were little short of astonishing. Over 75 per cent thought of social work as for anybody, irrespective of financial need.

The answers to a further question, "Under what conditions would YOU seek help from a social worker?" supplemented the above. According to the Welfare Federation report, only 116 of the 700 women questioned—16 per cent—said they would *not* go to a social worker under any circumstances. "However," the report says, "78 per cent of these same 116 had answered the previous question by saying that social work was for everybody. And of the 22 who said they would go to a social worker only as a last resort, 17 said social work was for everybody."[1]

The Plain Dealer, discussing these replies, reports:

Only 18 per cent named need of financial help [as the condition under which they themselves would seek help from a social worker]. Family problems—not financial— were mentioned by 25 per cent of the women. Personal problems were mentioned by three per cent, combined family and personal problems by eight per cent. Twenty per cent said they did not know what conditions would take them to a social worker.

On both questions there were substantial differences between answers of the wealthiest and poorest classes. More women of the well-to-do classes tended to think social work was for poor people. The poor people tended more to think social work was for everyone.

---

[1] Overmyer, Richard P., Here's the Score in Cleveland.

Although 63 per cent of the women in the topmost economic layer thought social work was for everyone, only 36 per cent of this class could think of any condition which would bring them personally to ask help of a social worker. In the bottom layer of the economic scale, 79 per cent thought social work was for everyone. Sixty-seven per cent found some home, personal or financial problem which would cause them to ask help of a social worker.

Five Cleveland social agencies now accept fees from people given service and able to pay for it. They are the Institute of Family Service, the Jewish Family Service Association, the Cleveland Guidance Center, Children's Services (formerly called the Humane Society) and the Youth Bureau.

Miss Helen W. Hanchette, executive director of the Institute of Family Service, said paying clients had increased 300 per cent in a year, although accepting client fees was a new practice.

William I. Lacy, executive director of Children's Services, said people who paid fees for it valued social welfare service more.

Strong contrasts appeared in answers rejecting social work as a help. Top and bottom economic classes stacked up this way in these answers:

	Highest income group	Lowest income group
Social work as a "last resort"......	6%	2%
Social work under no conditions....	44%	8%

Among the family problems women thought would bring them to ask a social worker's help, marital problems were mentioned only by one per cent, a low point equaled only by housing difficulties. Dr. [R. Clyde] White said this was probably due to a gap in the women's information on welfare work. "Husband-wife conflict is one of the problems

which most often create a need for the help of a professional social worker," Dr. White said. "The experience of
social agencies certainly shows that. But answers on these
questions show Clevelanders have pretty well outgrown the
fallacious idea that social work is simply another name for
relief."

Poll findings agree with actual experience of the Institute
of Family Service. "Only 10 per cent of the past year's
clients came because of financial need," said Miss Hanchette, "and some of these were merely inexperienced in
managing a home. They needed help on budgeting and
buying, not added money, to become self-sufficient. This
group was overshadowed by the 27 per cent who came for
help on family relationships."

Five questions[1] aimed to test the public's acquaintance with specific resources in situations calling for
casework. The Plain Dealer's write-up of the replies
to two of these indicates the trend of the findings.

Pastors and welfare workers are equally good at ironing
out family quarrels, Greater Cleveland women think, according to the latest replies in the Welfare Federation's
poll of public opinion. Each won one-third of the first
choices when women were asked: "Suppose you know a
couple whose quarreling is so serious that it is affecting
their children. Where do you think they could get help?"

Only two per cent of the women named "Mr. Anthony,"
the radio's adviser to the lovelorn. Biting or just barely
printable remarks about "Mr. Anthony" were made by an
equal number of pollees. Psychiatrists got eight per cent of
the first choices, doctors seven per cent and lawyers five
per cent.

Ministers won only one-fifth the first choices on a
similar question on adolescent child problems. Here social

[1] See questions 4, 5, 6, 7, and 8, pp. 96–97.

workers were picked by well over half the women as the best source of help. This question was: "Suppose you were the parent of a fourteen-year-old boy or girl who was running wild and getting out of your control. From whom would you seek help?"

Strung out behind the clergy and welfare agents were newspaper columnists (who were chosen by less than one per cent), policemen (one per cent), school principals (fourteen per cent) and political leaders or councilmen (who got no first choices at all).

"Close linking of pastors and social workers can often solve better the home frictions brought to each profession," said Miss Helen W. Hanchette, executive secretary of the Institute of Family Service. "Courage to meet a difficult situation may come from talking over a problem with a religious leader," she said. "At the same time, there is a trend among forward-looking pastors to use social agencies so that members of their congregations will become better adjusted and stronger members of the community."

Howard M. Wells, pastor of the First Presbyterian Church of East Cleveland and chairman of the Welfare Federation's casework council, said, "Social workers do not infringe on the work of the minister. They supplement and strengthen it. The average pastor can give only friendly, common sense advice. I am profoundly grateful that in Cleveland we have so many skillful social workers to turn to for help on problems needing more technical knowledge."

Commenting on the large number of women looking first to their pastor, Rev. A. J. Murphy, director of the Catholic Charities Bureau, said, "It is encouraging that, despite city living and the breakdown of neighborliness, a big percentage of people still turn to the church for counsel on family problems. This indicates that the church still does possess the vitality traditionally attributed to it in dealing with problems affecting the home."

Dr. R. Clyde White, chairman of the poll analysis board, concluded that Clevelanders showed by their poll replies that they knew of agencies appropriate to their problems and accepted them.

"This," he said, "fulfills one of the main aims of the opinion sampling job: to find out how well Cleveland, an advanced center of social welfare work, has been told the story of modern health and welfare techniques."

A study of all these questions and answers in the Cleveland Poll indicates that most Cleveland women have a warm and friendly feeling toward social work; that, when presented with a specific situation and with a description of the casework service which would meet it, they favored such a service overwhelmingly; that the majority knew casework services existed, but that a smaller percentage knew where to find them, or where to find persons or agencies who could direct them to any needed service.

The poll showed, too, that all the Cleveland papers considered the project newsworthy, and that one paper thought attitudes toward social work significant enough to deserve a series of seven signed articles.

We have no way of knowing if this poll—which queried women only—represents the feelings of the men of Cleveland, too. But an added experiment indicates that it may be generally representative.

A CHILDREN'S QUESTIONNAIRE

A member of our Advisory Committee, Mrs. Lucia J. Bing, suggested that a questionnaire to children, especially in neighborhoods or groups which had been widely exposed to casework, would throw light not only on their own but also on family attitudes. With the co-operation of the principal of the Tremont Public School, Pearl Monks, and the psychologist of the Detention Home, Edith Dombey, the following little questionnaire was devised.

1. Have you ever thought about the work you would like to do when you leave school and are ready to earn your own living? What would you like to do best?
2. There are people whose job it is to help other people who are in trouble. Do you know any such people who have helped families, as for example—(a) when some one is out of work (b) when some one dies (c) or when there is quarreling and unhappiness. Under what circumstances did you know them?
3. Have you or your family or your neighbors ever had any such help? In what ways?
4. Do you think it is a good idea to pay salaries from the Community Fund or from public taxes to welfare workers who spend their time and skill in helping people in trouble? Give reasons.
5. Would you like to be a welfare worker (sometimes called social worker) to help people in trouble? Give your reasons.

In all, 55 children filled out this questionnaire—36 in the 6-a grade in the public school, all between eleven and fourteen years of age; and 19 in the Detention Home, ranging in grade from fourth to twelfth and in age from twelve to seventeen.

The number of children who filled out the questionnaire is in itself too small to give us data of statistical significance. Yet in view of the larger poll's findings, the children's answers have a special interest.

No one inquiry on the questionnaire called for a direct opinion about social work; but the survey of all the answers and comment on any one schedule did show the child's thoughts or feelings.

Of the 36 public school children, 35 approved of social work and social workers, and one had a slight feeling against them. Of the 19 Detention Home children, 11 were for and 8 were against. Three of these 8 expressed mixed feelings. For example, a seventeen-year-old high-school girl (in the Detention Home because of immorality and pregnancy), who knew a social worker "in my own case of home troubled conditions," says, "Yes and no!" in answer both to the question about paying salaries to welfare workers, and to the one as to whether she would like to be a welfare worker. "Yes," she says, "if it really is to help people who are in trouble . . . being in the Detention Home I have heard many stories of girls who are being sent away. I do not know their cases so I cannot judge that. But I think a girl in trouble should be helped as much as possible and not pulled apart."

A child's general feeling of approval or disapproval of the social worker or social work may be only a reflection of a family attitude. Some of the questions, however, brought ingenuous answers, clearly first hand—for instance, the question "Do you think it is a good idea to pay salaries from the Community Fund or public taxes to welfare workers who spend their time and skill in helping people in trouble? Give reasons."

To this all but six children answered yes. Some understood the question to be a choice of the source of payment, and of those who did many preferred taxes.

Five of the six children who thought social workers should not be paid were in the Detention Home. The comments of those ranged from an outright, "No, I don't" to conditional ones such as, "If a worker is really interested in helping a child better himself, but in my estimation workers give no help whatsoever. Perhaps some do, but the majority don't." One seventeen-year-old wrote, "Most welfare workers are wealthy and need no funds for supporting themselves. Social workers do welfare work to pass the time away since they have nothing else to do."

But such answers were the exception, even among the Detention Home children. A boy of fourteen, detained because of attempted burglary, thought social workers should be paid, because "They take their time to help people in trouble when they could do something for themself." Other reasons given were, "Because some day you may have to look to that same person for help." "[They] help children to get homes. They help them to get a good job. Also help them to get a good start in life."

The public school children gave some of the above and other reasons for pay. "They work so they should be paid for their work." "Yes, because where else would they get their money?" "Yes. Well they help us like the firemen they help us if there is a fire they tried to put the fire out."

The question which most directly brought out the feeling about social workers was: "Would you like to be a welfare worker (sometimes called a social worker) to help people in trouble? Give your reasons."

Here again though the yes or no proportions have no significance, some of the comments are revealing.

Among the Detention Home children, an incorrigible fourteen-year-old girl replied, "No! I would rather mind my own business than everyone elses." A seventeen-year-old girl, detained for "loitering," says, "Yes. Providing people were actually *in* trouble. I think that more social workers try to make a 'mountain out of a molehill,' I know that problems can be worked out in one's own family circle. Why do they insist on separating members of the family. If only one social worker would try to solve family problems within the home instead of including another family."

This opinion, like most of those among the Detention Home children, grew out of experience with social workers, including probation officers. One truant girl of sixteen did not try to answer the question but used the space to protest, "Why should a child be placed in a place like this when he or she's mother is sick and there is other child . . . I don't think it is fair."

The thoughts of the public school children about becoming social workers were less tethered to their own direct experience than were those of the Detention Home children, even though many of the families of the former—15 out of 36—had had relief or other social work help in time of trouble. Their replies ranged on the looser guide lines of their more temporary wishes or their fresh reactions to ideas met for the first time. "No, I want to be a stewardess more than anything else." "Yes, it makes you feel good to know you helped some one that needed help." "No. Some people will not like you when you try to help them. I don't know if I would like it." "Yes. Because

I'd be helping people and they are grateful and if your in trouble sometime they might help you." "No, because I don't think I was a person made out for that kind of work and I don't think I would like it." "Yes. Because they helped our family when we were pretty bad off. And I would like to help a poor family too." "No. I just don't like that kind of work. I would rather help pay for the social worker's wages."

As we have said, this collection of children's thoughts about social work and social workers is too small to have any statistical significance. Yet it is significant when even little children recognize that a social worker needs to be a certain kind of person; that she should be paid for her work; that the work itself, like a fireman's, is important; that it may be unpleasant ("because some people will not like you when you try to help them"). It is significant, too, when children express some of the very aims a caseworker might have put forth—a little girl's statement, for instance, "that problems can be worked out in one's own circle"; or another, that "a girl in trouble should be helped . . . not pulled apart."

Such spontaneous *knowing* should hearten the caseworker and help her to take for granted a general capacity for public understanding of her work.

The children's questionnaires bear out the findings of the larger poll, which showed a general friendliness toward social work far greater than Cleveland social workers had believed possible.

Underrating Public Goodwill

The caseworkers' expectation of a lack of friendliness stems from various roots: the knowledge that much past casework was inadequate; that much present-day casework falls short of the best professional standards; that many positions requiring professional skills are staffed by untrained or inadequately trained workers; that even trained workers sometimes lack the right personality for the job. The memory of past criticism also aggravates her expectancy of bad opinion—especially the memory of the attacks of politicians during the depression years, and the bitterness of public welfare clients, suffering under the corrosion of scanty and often callously administered relief.

A poll taken in that period would doubtless have shown much less friendliness, perhaps even an enmity to social work. But Cleveland has apparently outgrown those attitudes faster than social workers have outgrown their fear or expectations of such attitudes.

George Gallup, director of the American Institute of Public Opinion, believes that the public is frequently far ahead of where the specialist thinks it is. "I often," he writes, "hear men in public life say that such-and-such a program for social betterment has to be postponed or that you have to 'go easy' with it because 'public opinion isn't ready for it.' A lot of the time that is pure bunk. The common man has more liberal-minded ideas about social questions than his leaders credit him with. At least that is my conclusion after ten years of polling the public on thousands of public issues." And again, "Sometimes the public has to mark time until its leaders catch up with the procession."[1]

[1] Gallup, George, "The People Are with You," in Channels, July-August, 1945.

It is possible that a poll taken even during the period of bitterest attacks on social workers would have shown something different from the social workers' appraisal of public attitudes about them or their work. Or it might simply have shown that there is little deeply rooted opinion one way or the other. A Cleveland public relations specialist, Paul Einstein, says that most of the business executives he meets have no conception of what social work, including casework, does, and no feelings for or against it, except as these feelings happen to get aroused. "Their opinions when they have them often depend on whether they identify social work with certain public issues or parties. Those who disliked the New Deal, for instance, were inclined to dislike social work because they identified it with the New Deal. And vice versa." He further reported it as his experience that people's opinions were often easily changed. "A man may change his mind out of respect for the opinion of someone else; or because the subject is presented in a way to appeal to his prejudices or his preferences." And he cited an instance in a community fund campaign in which a reluctant giver who happened also to be opposed to the public relief program, needed nothing more than the question "Do you want it all done by the government?" to make him decide he was for private philanthropy. Another man might be just as easily swayed to vote for a good public appropriation by some such emotionally flavored question as "Do you wish it left to the caprice of private philanthropy?"

The findings of the Cleveland polls might tempt caseworkers to assume that all is well with public attitudes toward casework in that city; and that, with such assurance, they could sweep ahead on the momentum of general public liking. True, they can go farther ahead than they had previously thought. But caseworkers would be the first to say that, though public opinion there is kind, it is not exactly knowledgeable. For the poll answers give little evidence of any deep or wide understanding of casework. Caseworkers still have before them the task of helping public knowledge catch up with public friendliness.

How then, we may ask, do they go about this task? And what is Cleveland's casework field doing there, not only agency by agency—but through the Welfare Federation—to provide accurate knowledge of its work and of its aims?

CHAPTER VI
AVENUES TO PUBLIC INTEREST

EARLIER chapters have discussed the value of the individual caseworker as an interpreter of her agency, and as a source of public knowledge and opinion about casework. But this one-by-one way to public understanding, potent as it is, even at its best falls short. For an agency is more than its staff. It is the sum of its staff, its clients, its board, its committees, its volunteers; of its interlockings into community life; and of its aims. And not only of today's components, for old aspirations, old policies, old virtues and errors are also a part of it; and these carry their impetus into present opinion, just as present policies and qualities will affect future attitudes.

Thus many individuals and many abstract forces contribute to the public's knowledge and impressions of the casework of a single agency or of casework in general. Sometimes the knowledge, nurtured by good programs or good ventures of public information, approaches accuracy. Often the impressions, allowed to crop up at random, lie wide of the mark.

The interpretation of casework is left almost entirely to the local agencies and councils of agencies. In the national offices this field is less well equipped for securing public understanding than any other branch of health and welfare work. Movements like the Boy Scouts or Girl Scouts, or the National Tuberculosis

Association or the Young Men's Christian Associations, have well-staffed public relations departments in their national offices. But such major casework associations as the Family Service Association of America, the Child Welfare League of America, and the American Public Welfare Association, employ no publicity or public relations specialists. Even the American Red Cross, with many caseworkers in its Home Service division, devotes little publicity to its casework. The Family Service Association of America did, for a period of about two years, employ a public relations consultant; but when its budget had to be cut, the public relations function was dropped.[1]

AGENCY PUBLIC RELATIONS

In recent years, especially in the family field, local casework agencies and groups of agencies have begun to consider interpretation an important part of their function. The extent to which they translate this idea into action varies from community to community, from agency to agency. Some agencies, especially in these short-staffed days, depend for their public relations almost entirely upon the quality of their work. They do this on the premise that good casework by itself will generate sound opinion; that through it the clients, their friends, and those who refer clients to agencies will know and judge the usefulness of any service.

Other agencies feel that they must make their work known to more people than those who happen to come or to be sent to their doors. These agencies—to widen

---

[1] Since this was written the Family Service Association of America has engaged a full-time public relations director.

their usefulness, to increase their financial support and the support of social measures which their experience sponsors—make what use they can of various avenues to public interest: the printed word in pamphlets, bulletins, and reports; co-operation with such community resources for publicity as the newspaper and the radio; meetings, institutes, and informal talks; and demonstration by special projects.

How does a casework agency organize itself for its public relations task? Does it employ a specialist to create public understanding of its work? Has it an active interpretation or public relations committee? Or does it depend on the chance ability or talent for publicity and interpretation of the executive or some gifted volunteer or board member?

To seek the answers to some of these questions the Family Service Association of America in 1944–1945 sent a questionnaire to its private member agencies. The answers showed that only 10 of 216 reporting agencies employed staff members assigned to the job of telling their various publics what the agencies really do and what they stand for.[1] And only 116, or little more than half, reported committees responsible for any continuing phase of interpretation.

No recent analogous figures are available for the children's or the public welfare agencies. But it seems safe to guess that they are less active in working for general public understanding or the understanding of more closely related publics than is the private family

[1] At present writing (1947) 13 of the 234 member agencies of the Family Service Association of America employ such staff members. Of these, one agency has a public relations staff of six full time workers; six agencies each employ one full time worker, and six agencies each a part time worker.

agency, which, goaded by the depression-born establishment of wide-scale public relief, had to plow its
way into public confidence if it was to survive.

In Cleveland, both in the Family Service Association and in the Jewish Family Service Association, the
importance of good public relations has long been
recognized. These agencies have developed a sense of
responsibility for interpretation in their staffs, clerical
as well as professional. Their board members and
volunteers take an active—though not necessarily
sustained—part in working for public understanding
of some phases of the agencies' work. They do this
sometimes by committee participation, sometimes by
participation—under professional caseworkers' guidance—in services to clients. This latter activity is
rather highly developed in the Jewish Family Service
Association, especially through its Big Brother and
Big Sister Associations. Both agencies publish bulletins and carry on other publicity ventures.

Cleveland's Family Service Association is one of
the 10 member agencies of the Family Service Association of America that reported in 1944–1945 em-
ploying a public relations specialist. Its present educational secretary (who began as a caseworker) has
for over twenty years been in charge of agency
publicity, including the annual report, the bulletin
Family Affairs, the arrangements for annual and
other meetings, and has also been responsible for
maintaining close contacts with newspaper reporters
and columnists. (The agency's close working relationship with newspapers is discussed in the following
chapter.)

The employment of such a specialist in itself signals the agency's awareness of the importance of community partnership; and, of course, it furthers such partnership. It makes possible a continuing relationship with newspapers, radio, and other channels of communication; and with special groups in the community. It facilitates the discovery of talent for interpretation among staff members, board members, and volunteers, and helps provide outlets for such talent. What is more, a single casework agency effectively presenting its own work, also advances the understanding of other casework agencies in the community. This holds especially true in Cleveland where all the agencies work closely together.

Although no other Cleveland casework agency employed a public relations specialist at the time of our study, some of them carried on effective interpretation. The Jewish Family Service Association—especially through its various committees; through well-sustained organization of volunteers in its Big Brother and Big Sister Associations; and through its bulletin Family Welfare, other pamphlets, and articles in the bulletins and other publications of Temples—has for years kept the Jewish community of Cleveland in close touch with its aims and its development. It works closely, too, with non-Jewish organizations toward their common aims. One year, 1940, it met with the Family Service Association of Cleveland in a joint annual meeting.

Of the other Cleveland casework organizations whose structure for public relations was considered in our study, only three had interpretation committees. Some of the others, however, put careful thought—

through presentation to special groups, such as doctors, churches, schools and clubs, especially the parent-teacher associations—upon making their work known, though for the most part their activity in interpretation was haphazard. And some agencies reported it their policy to avoid interpretation and publicity, so as not to draw more clients than their staff or budget could care for.

AGENCY BULLETINS

Bulletins and annual reports are among the most effective ways of keeping members and friends of an agency in touch with its work. We choose here for sampling the Family Service Association's bulletin, Family Affairs. This bulletin, which comes out about four times a year, has a wide distribution. Its 2,000 copies reach—among others—life members, volunteers, committee members, ministers, teachers, other social agencies and civic leaders in the community. Some 75 copies of each issue are sent to the public library for distribution to its branches, and to the libraries of public schools.

Casework is its constant theme, but each issue selects some one phase, discusses it, and usually illustrates it with case stories. Thus one issue, called Chemistry and Casework, built about marriage problems, begins with the following comment:

Just as hydrogen and oxygen combine to make water, so it takes a combination of elements to make a marital problem. Many individuals, troubled because of threatened breakdown in their marriage, come to the Institute of

Family Service[1] for assistance. The caseworker's job is to try to help them find the good elements in their "formula" and combine them to produce a sounder way of living for the family.

All of us are combinations of good and bad elements, strengths and weaknesses; and we react accordingly to the every day tasks of our lives. We may have the strength to face one difficulty with courage and foresight, but pressure from a different point bowls us over. Individuals involved in marital unhappiness may have faced other life situations with equanimity but trouble in their marriage leaves them gasping.

Sometimes the pressure which pushes a marriage toward explosion comes from outside sources—unemployment, illness, lack of education, personal catastrophe. Other times the pressure is inside the individuals. In either case, a successful solution requires locating and removing or modifying the cause.

The bulletin then uses two case stories, showing different marriage problems, and how the caseworker helped the couples work toward their solution. After this it comments:

The case worker cannot always be successful as a catalytic agent—sometimes the elements of a marriage just don't mix. Where we are successful it is the result of painstakingly learning *why* the person acts as he does—what he expects of marriage—what he demands for himself and is willing to give his partner, how badly he wants his marriage to be successful.

The case worker can help with external problems of environment and finances and with internal problems of the personality if individuals are willing to struggle to find and use their own strength, to overcome their weaknesses.

[1] Now Family Service Association.

Each partner must be willing to compromise, to learn and understand the other, to find the values of marriage greener than the grass outside.

An issue titled Can Everybody Work? discusses various phases of the problem of helping people not employed to prepare themselves for work.

We must recognize first that if they are to be hired, they must be ready to compete in industry and to fulfill the requirements placed on the jobs that are available. If our efforts to help them get work include special preparation for that work, they must be capable of taking full advantage of what is offered.

The bulletin then tells briefly about a number of persons who came to the agency for help with employment problems: for example, a middle-aged pharmacist who "drinks and has trouble with his wife, or has trouble with his wife and drinks"; "a 54-year-old gardener who over a period of years has worked in a protected job where the evidences of his mental illness have been minimized," but who finally "went berserk and threatened his employer. As a result he was sent to a State Hospital from which he has recently been released. His age, his limited work background and his mental state make it difficult for him to secure work."

After suggesting the many kinds of people, young and old, ill and well, who come with employment problems, the writer comments:

More often than not, if any one of these approached you for a job, you would question his ability to work efficiently. *Our job* becomes one of helping these people straighten themselves out to a point where you would want to hire them. We must help them no matter what their color, race, creed, age, skill or mental or physical handicap. When you want to hire one of them, you expect him to be ready for work—getting him ready is our job.

We have an equally important job, that of *keeping* people at work. Here in contrast to dealing with the unemployed, we are concerned with people who are employed. Generally speaking, their problems center in the need for someone to help them make plans for the future, to help them straighten out difficulties at home, to help them deal with questions they may have about themselves. They are the people who meet the requirements of industry, who, on the surface, have the physical, mental and educational background to do a job and do it well. . . .

. . . it is hard for people who are inwardly disturbed about themselves or conditions at home to work efficiently despite the fact that they might try to work diligently. . .

The job then is two-fold, helping employed people keep their equilibrium and stay on the job and helping people who for some special reason, not always readily determined, do not have a job, prepare themselves for work and find work that they are able to do.

One of the most recent issues of Family Affairs carries the title Troubles, Mental and Emotional. Because this subject greatly concerns caseworkers everywhere, and because a good many agencies struggle to help people understand just how casework relates itself to the various psychiatric facilities in a community, and what the caseworker can and cannot do, it seems worth while to quote a large part of this issue of Family Affairs, including some of the case illustrations.

The social worker is not a psychiatrist. Yet of the thousands of people who each year bring a wide range of problems to the agency for help, a sizable number are obviously suffering from mental or emotional difficulties. These difficulties vary from serious mental illness to mild emotional disturbances, with some severe anxieties which untreated may lead to mental breakdown. Because people live for the most part in families, their troubles in turn are a source of anxiety to those closest to them.

How can the family case worker help?

1. The case worker can help the patient or his family understand something of the nature of mental illness, that such illness is not necessarily incurable; can stress the importance of early diagnosis; can help both the patient and his family make adjustments within the home which will ease the situation for all concerned.

2. Knowing community resources, the case worker can help the family see the need for early treatment, can tell them about different forms of psychiatric help, and can encourage the continued use of psychiatric help when once arranged for.

3. The case worker can treat many temporary emotional disturbances and the less severe forms of neurotic difficulties, thereby stabilizing the client and his family.

The case worker's first step is often to share with her clients such of her own understanding of mental and emotional problems as will allay exaggerated fears. Being neither doctor nor psychiatrist, she does not make medical or psychiatric diagnoses. She does recognize symptoms that are danger signals and has recourse to medical and psychiatric consultation as needed. She can often give reassurance as to possible cure, can change old-time notions such as "you've got to lock 'em up."

She can sometimes break down prejudices or fears regarding psychiatrists, the notion that they are just for "crazy people." "What do psychiatrists do?" "What kind of people are they?" "How much do they charge?" "Will they give me that awful shock treatment?" These are some of the questions that come to the social worker for answer.

This preparing the way for psychiatric help is an important piece of work with many clients. While alert to the dangers of delay, the case worker also recognizes the danger of increasing a person's fears through a hasty referral for which he is in no way ready.

Encouraging clients to accept institutional or custodial care when it is most needed and when it is available is frequently necessary. A mother often hesitates to press for placement of a mentally retarded child until she comes to understand how such a child kept at home can affect her other children; how, too, such a retarded child may improve and be happier in a training school where he will not suffer from too great competition. Facilities for the mentally retarded are woefully lacking but the case worker, knowing both the family and the social problems created in the community, may sometimes be able to speed up placement. . . .

"Mr. Burt" could not bring himself to have his wife probated though he knew what her disturbed mind was doing to their three young children. She staged terrible scenes at home and at times wandered off, leaving him for days to be both father and mother. The older boy was becoming a problem at school. The little three year old was having temper tantrums like her mother's. One day, after a particularly bad scene with his wife, he came to the office again in despair. "I've just got to do something," he said, "but I can't stand it to have my wife arrested like a common drunk. What can I do?"

When the new voluntary commitment to Hoover Pavilion was explained he was greatly interested and went home at once to tell his wife about it and get her consent. She was an intelligent woman who knew that she really needed help. She signed the papers and is already making some progress at the hospital. The children are under the care of one of the agency's supervised homemakers. Mr. Burt, though still concerned about his wife's situation, at least feels now that things are moving, that there may in time again be a happy future for them all.

With "Joe Davis" the case was different, for him the only way out was to be probated. The personnel manager of a big plant where he was working telephoned the agency to ask what could be done. Back several months from overseas, Joe was acting queer on the job, spoiling materials, quarreling with the other workmen, often sullenly refusing to work. He was acting so ugly that they were afraid to fire him. Unsuccessful attempts had been made to get in touch with his mother with whom he lived.

The case worker agreed to take over and certainly spent a busy day. She succeeded in locating his family and found them aware of his condition but afraid to do anything about it. The papers that should admit him directly to a veterans' hospital were missing. His mother and sister accompanied the worker down to Probate Court and swore out the necessary warrant. His employer was called and cautioned to hold Joe until he could be picked up. After psychiatric examination at Court he could then be turned over to the veterans' hospital, where he is still receiving treatment.

Few of the veterans coming in today present problems so serious. Most of their difficulties are emotional rather than mental, centering in readjustment to civilian life and having their origin in situations definitely pre-war. . . .

Not only returned servicemen get alarmed about themselves and question their sanity. The wife of a big business executive, a college graduate and former teacher, came in recently to the district office terribly upset. "I must be losing my mind," she said, "I'm getting so I can't stand my husband, my children, or my in-laws. Everything they do drives me crazy. Have you got any nice padded cells around?" she said with a half laugh.

In going into the details of what things bothered her most, she talked at length of her husband's "lack of system." He was always being late to meals, didn't keep appointments with her. The children were careless though she had spent her life trying to train them properly. Questions followed in which she brought out her own almost impossibly high standard of housekeeping, the too great demands she made on her children, her strict adherence to a system which allowed for no exceptions, the impossible schedule she imposed on the whole household.

"Has it ever occurred to you," asked the case worker, "to question your own system of life? It may suit your particular temperament, but does it fit others who are different from you? Have you thought that you might possibly be too rigid at times?" For a moment she just looked at the case worker, then said, "That is an entirely new idea to me. I want to go home and think it over. But I'll be back." . . .

To many people it is easier and less frightening to go to a social worker than to a psychiatrist. Where the need for a psychiatrist is urgent, the case worker can make the necessary arrangements at once. Where it is not needed she may save valuable time all around. And always she can be a source of strength to the family.

PARTICIPATION THROUGH VOLUNTEER SERVICES

The understanding gained both by using services and by participation in the program of the agency which provides them helps to create an informed and interested public. The value of word-of-mouth endorsement—by which one client who has been helped sends another, or one referral source, pleased with the help given to some previously referred person, sends someone else—is taken for granted.

But the interest and goodwill which grow out of certain other forms of identification with an agency's work call for comment. Such identification may come about through various volunteer services, whether on committees, or in direct services to clients. In Cleveland widespread membership on boards and committees is woven into the whole pattern of social and civic work—so much so that Cleveland is often referred to as a "committee town." Indeed, a journalist, writing lightly but with meaning, once said, "The good Clevelander before turning out his light to get into bed asks himself, 'Have I co-operated today or have I failed?'"[1]

In the Welfare Federation every division of social work has a council composed of both professional and lay members—each with its own professional secretary—who carry on the program of the council through diverse committees. Together they take part in various projects which, even when they deal with such esoteric subject matter as casework, are considered to be of community concern. One committee which serves all the Federation councils and agencies, including the casework agencies, is the Advisory Committee of the Central Volunteer Bureau of the Welfare Federation. Its function is to promote the use of volunteers in agencies, advise with professional workers on their volunteer programs, and raise the standards of volunteer service.

The use of volunteers on committees or in campaigns for funds or for legislation or in projects of community service, is more common in casework

[1] Duffus, R. L., "Cleveland—Paternalism in Excelsis," in New Republic, April 24, 1928.

agencies than is their use in direct service to clients.

Time was when all the work of social agencies was done by volunteers. With the growth of professionalism, their use has dwindled or greatly changed. This is naturally true in the casework field. In many agencies they are used only for a few specific tasks—such as taking a child for his weekly visit to a clinic, or providing transportation, or an occasional treat, or friendly visits to old persons. In some agencies they are not used at all. And, although they are frequently expected to have some responsibility for agency interpretation, all too often they get little first-hand knowledge of casework and little, if any, training for interpretation.

Some agencies feel strongly that volunteers can with training and supervision be used effectively as casework aides in a way satisfying to them and valuable to the agency. In Cleveland both the Family Service Association and the Jewish Family Service Association regard the use and training of volunteers as valuable and important. Since 1924 the former has had an active Volunteer Advisory Committee whose duties have been to stimulate and co-ordinate all agency volunteer activities. Recently the Family Service Association has again added to its staff for half time a trained secretary on volunteer service, who is working both with the Volunteer Advisory Committee and with a small staff committee in defining the role of the volunteer in a family agency and in selecting, training, and fitting her into the casework program.

The Jewish Family Service Association, with its affiliates the Big Brother and Big Sister Associations, has for a long time used volunteers, giving them a course of training and careful supervision. One of the meetings of the Big Sister Association, for example, had as its agenda a caseworker's presentation of the story of Rosalind, a troubled ten-year-old; an account by the volunteer of her part in helping Rosalind; comments by a psychologist at the child's school, and by the case supervisor of a children's agency; and questions and discussion by the Big Sisters. This particular story was not a story of successful casework used to show the volunteers how much could be done for a child. It was a picture of a little girl whose whole dreary childhood called for a kind of help beyond the knowledge and skills of caseworkers of that time. But it helped every volunteer who attended the meeting to understand what might cause a particular child—and thus, any child—to be unlovable and unloving; and to be unable to get along in the world. It showed, too, how much the Big Sister had been able to do, and how little. And how what she did dovetailed into the caseworker's plans.

Because this story of Rosalind is valuable as teaching and training material for volunteers, and for that matter for caseworkers, too, we are presenting it as Appendix B.[1]

When volunteers receive training and come to know and understand casework, they become valuable spokesmen and can forward both the understanding of casework and various community measures which the experience of casework may sponsor.

[1] See p. 231.

CASEWORK UNITES TO TELL ITS STORY

Casework agencies now tend more and more to work together on undertakings to secure public use and interest. These joint enterprises find easier access to the various channels of publicity than do those of single agencies. But no one would suggest any slackening in the efforts by individual agencies for good public relations. Every enterprising agency, of course, wishes to keep and deepen the interests of its special groups and of as much of the general public as possible. The separate agency can often do things which cannot be done in concert, and vice versa. But every good multiple-agency or federation approach to the public smooths the paths for the single agency.

Some of the best public relations for casework have been established not by separate agencies but by groups of agencies, often carrying on projects under the aegis of councils or federations of social agencies. The war and some of the war's-end problems greatly stimulated these joint undertakings. They ranged from descriptive directories of all the social agencies in a community to special bulletins or leaflets about some particular service—such as the work of family service agencies—for distribution to USO camps or veterans' centers; from the carefully organized after-hour volunteer work given to draft boards by case-workers to special campaigns for foster homes; from research projects and demonstrations of the usefulness of certain kinds of services to institutes open to the general public.

Cleveland—especially fortunate in active research and public relations departments in its Welfare Federation—has carried on a number of these enterprises which cut across agency lines, both in connection with war activities and independent of them. They all aimed to increase the usefulness and the support of the city's agencies, and were, as well, excellent public relations projects. Some, such as the Health and Welfare Directory, or the all-day institutes carried on each year[1] and drawing an attendance of over a thousand, include some presentation of casework along with that of other social and health activities of the city. Others, such as the establishment of the Tremont Service Center and the War Homes for Children campaign, had to do exclusively with the field of casework.

We select these last two for detailed description here because they illustrate the close interweaving of active public interest with the provision of specific services.

THE TREMONT SERVICE BUREAU

The Tremont Service Bureau grew out of a study[2] made in 1934–1935 of a part of Cleveland known as the Tremont area. This neighborhood, with some 15,000 people living within 64 city blocks, was then notorious for a high juvenile delinquency rate. Although not far from the city's center, its topography and limited transportation facilities isolated it. Its large foreign composition—made up of Poles, Russians, Ruthenians, Slovaks, and other Slavic stocks— further separated it from Cleveland's cultural life.

[1] See p. 148.
[2] Hendry, Charles, and Svendsen, Margaret, Between Spires and Stacks. Welfare Federation of Cleveland, 1936.

This survey uncovered many problems besides juvenile delinquency. "It was evident," wrote Katherine Clark,[1] reviewing the findings, "that with congestion in homes, more recreational opportunities outside of homes were needed; with houses crowded on the land, more open play spaces were needed; with high tuberculosis rates, more emphasis on food and rest and better housing was needed; with tolerance and tradition of delinquency, new controls and new approaches were needed; with an academic high school serving youth who would never go to college, adjustment of curriculum was needed; and with the bad reputation of the area, pride and community morale were needed. Among these needs was the need for a co-ordinated attack upon all these problems by all the forces—particularly the social and educational agencies."

How Cleveland attacked these various needs and reduced the Tremont area's delinquency, tuberculosis and infant mortality rates, as well as the cultural conflicts between various nationality groups, is a part of our story of public relations only so far as it affects casework and the use of casework in this troubled neighborhood.

The area study recommended, among other things, that for an experimental period all casework services be consolidated in a single center. As a result, in 1937, the specialized agencies—the Family Service Association, the Catholic Youth Service Bureau (Big Sisters at that time), the Youth Bureau (Girls' Bureau at that time), the Children's Bureau, and the Humane

[1] Review of the Tremont Project, presented to the Case Work Council, Welfare Federation of Cleveland, 1943.

Society—withdrew, and the Tremont Service Bureau, a single general casework agency, came into being.

The Bureau was housed in the Tremont Center, a conveniently located building, which also housed other community services. The Well Baby Clinic of the City Health Department met at the Center twice a week; the Visiting Nurse came every day; a Juvenile Court probation officer came once a week; and the City Relief Department, and the Aid to Dependent Children both used the joint office space for interviewing. Then, too, the Day Nursery of the Merrick House Settlement was situated right behind the Center, and co-operated closely with it.

Every good social survey becomes by its very process of inquiry, its contacts with leaders of many groups, and with many individuals, an instrument of interpretation. Its findings, in turn, become the material for further interpretation. The Tremont survey was no exception. Some 300 persons in the area and out, professional and lay, took part in it. All the key people in the area were interviewed, and the co-operation of schools, churches, and of the leaders of various nationality groups was secured. When the time came to put the survey's recommendations into effect, and to form a Community Council, the Welfare Federation knew just what persons to bring into it. Unlike many neighborhood councils where the planning is done by a group which the services never touch, nearly everyone in this area was affected by the survey's recommendations, and large numbers of persons came to feel a strong responsibility for them. Individuals, schools—parochial and public—housing project leaders, recreation leaders, the police, the churches, all referred families to the Bureau when some individual service seemed needed. A priest of one of the neighborhood's 12 churches told of a woman whom he urged to go to the Bureau. "You'll never hear from me again if I go to that place," she protested. "Oh yes I will," he replied, "because I'm a *part* of it."

The establishment and success of the Tremont Service Bureau illustrates the value of research and demonstration as tools of public relations. In this case it might be said to be almost too successful. The time came when the Federation believed that values of the Bureau's experience could be more far reaching if the Bureau were under the administration of the Family Service Association, to be used as a continuing laboratory for early case-finding and preventive service. Even though the proposed transfer would have caused little change in the operating policies developed while under Federation auspices, and even though all the co-ordinating and planning features of the project were to be continued, along with the joint office-space plan, the people in the Tremont area refused to accept the transfer. They thought of it as their own, as essential to their neighborhood as the improved health, housing, recreation, and other group-work resources established or encouraged by the recommendations of the survey.

But finally in 1946 a transfer was worked out, with agreement of area leaders. They recognized that the principal successful features of the Bureau which distinguished it in its early years were now part of the newly defined function of the Family Service Association; and that the transfer would increase the values both to the area and to Cleveland as a whole. The same name, Tremont Service Bureau, is continued, and an advisory committee with neighborhood representation is used, and the service continues to be a neighborhood service. Neighborhood leaders still regard it as their own.

Several other area projects of the Cleveland Welfare Federation would also provide material pertinent to a study of public relations. We selected the Tremont area for discussion because of its emphasis on the wide use of casework, as well as because of the quality of public relations which went into it; and because it illustrates vividly the use of demonstration as a force in public relations.

A Campaign for Foster Homes

Another Cleveland Welfare Federation project— the War Homes for Children campaign—also shows the effectiveness of an undertaking which cuts across agency lines in the casework field to provide a community service, and in so doing informs a wide public of a service the basis of which is casework.

In various parts of the country, even before the war, Protestant, Catholic, and Jewish foster home agencies working together pioneered in co-operative efforts to find foster homes for children. The war, crashing in upon family life everywhere, sharpening and increasing the need for foster homes, added the spur of patriotism to such joint appeals. In this atmosphere a number of cities carried on vigorous foster home campaigns.[1]

[1] Boston, Cleveland, Los Angeles, Milwaukee, New Orleans, Pittsburgh, Richmond (Virginia), and Syracuse (New York) reported such campaigns to the Child Welfare League of America.

We are reporting in some detail upon Cleveland's War Homes for Children campaign, partly because of its wide and effective spread, and partly because its basic material, though it uses the leverage of war and patriotism, would be as suggestive and stimulating to any group of agencies planning a joint search for foster homes today as during the war. Indeed, a study of its basic statement[1] reveals only an occasional reference to the war. And only a few of the children listed in the section "Typical War Home Children" had fathers in the armed forces.

This campaign used all possible channels to the public—the press, radio, bulletins, pamphlets, letters to interested individuals, and meetings. Some 64 items in newspapers, covering practically every day of the one-month period, contained news stories, editorials, feature articles, cartoons, and announcements. They appeared not only in Cleveland's three daily papers, but in special publications—neighborhood news, shopping news, foreign papers, religious papers, and suburban papers. Cleveland's five radio stations carried broadcasts and announcements. Ministers, priests, and rabbis appealed to their congregations and special groups, both from their pulpits and in special meetings.

Over 700 people attended the campaign's opening meeting—including boarding mothers, agency board members, agency staff members, and other interested persons. Two hundred and thirteen other meetings, large and small, reached luncheon clubs, religious, social and philanthropic groups, nationality groups, women's organizations, business organizations, lodges,

[1] See p. 140.

and parent-teacher associations. Besides, a statement of the aims of the campaign was made to the 40,000 spectators at the Charity Football Game, at the Cleveland Stadium.

The success of this one-month campaign for foster homes may be gauged from a report by the chairman of the campaign immediately after the drive closed.

Campaign statistics as of December 10 reveal that 1,140 leads or inquiries were received. Each one has been acknowledged by the campaign office. We feel that the results are very encouraging and worthwhile; 587, or 52%, were allocated to the agencies and 553 were withdrawn or rejected. Of this number [553], over 200 did not follow up their original inquiry, and the balance did not meet requirements or were not interested after the original interview. The cost of the campaign was slightly over $2,100 and was met from funds appropriated by the Welfare Federation.

One reason the campaign succeeded was, to be sure, the war psychology of the times, with its fusing of many disparate aims into a community-minded force for action. This strengthened and stirred many individuals to contribute to the winning of the war by activities or in channels not easily tapped in the less compulsive urgencies of peace. Another reason for the campaign's success was the quality of its well-prepared and well-written basic material. The following promotion statement—of which some 1,500 copies were distributed—provided sound information upon which the news stories, radio programs, pamphlets, speeches, and other material could be built, and it foresaw and answered many questions which potential foster parents might well ask.

General Information on War Homes for Children[1]

Over 400 children in Cleveland are now in critical need of homes. In addition, several hundred more should be placed in homes if there are enough private families willing to take care of them.

These are all children of broken homes, children of homes in which the parents have been seriously affected by any of the six D's—disease, death, divorce, desertion, drink, or disaster. Naturally all of these disrupters of family life have been much increased by the war, and the need for homes for the children of these broken families has become a critical war need.

PATRIOTIC SERVICE IN YOUR OWN HOME

It would be difficult to find a job of more importance to America than that of caring for children today so as to make better citizens tomorrow. You can render a truly patriotic service to your country by taking one of these children of broken homes into your family. Best of all, you can carry out this service in your own home.

THE KIND OF CHILDREN NEEDING HOMES

These are children of all nationalities, of all ages— babies, toddlers, grade-school children, and adolescents. Some are bright; some not so bright. Some are good; some have never had the chance to be good. Most are healthy; some are crippled or have disabilities which would be a challenge to those who wish to help the handicapped. Some are white; some colored. Some are Catholic, some Protestant, some Jewish. Some are pretty children, some plain. There are blondes, brunettes, redheads and in-betweens.

[1] Under auspices of the Welfare Federation.

These youngsters are alike in only one thing: each needs a home. Their own homes have been broken through circumstances they could do nothing to prevent.

All of these children have one or more relatives still living. Because of unfortunate conditions, their relatives cannot give them a home at present but remain interested in them and some day may be able to take care of them again. Such children are, therefore, not for adoption. They are to be "on loan" to those who can help them over a difficult period.

There are also some boys and girls of 'teen ages who are beginning to work and who need somewhere to live, who need someone to give them guidance, but who no longer consider themselves children. These youths pay their own board. What they need above all else is advice and affection from adults who will treat them as one of the family. There are, at present, several hundred boys and girls already receiving care of this type in the Cleveland area; there are also many more who are eligible for this type of care.

THE KIND OF PEOPLE NEEDED AS WAR-HOME PARENTS

What these children require is a normal, healthy, happy home life. They need homes with stable, normal, healthy people. They need a foster father as well as a foster mother. They need foster parents *both* of whom are truly interested in children and who are willing to spend the time and patience required to help a child become an honest, robust citizen.

These foster parents should have enough room in their homes and should have sufficient income for their own needs.

In some cases, widows or married women whose husbands are in Service can take care of one or two children, especially if there is some male relative who can be of help. Generally, however, the complete family is most desired.

FINANCIAL ARRANGEMENTS

Board is paid to cover the cost of a child's care. This varies from $20 to $30 a month, according to the child's age and sex. The agency will keep each child provided with clothing. This is good clothing. Every effort is made to see that a child is dressed like other children in the neighborhood.

The agency also provides medical care. Each child is given a thorough physical examination before placement. Routine check-ups are also given from time to time thereafter.

STATE LICENSING

By law the State requires that children be placed only in homes that measure up to a minimum standard, and therefore requires every foster home to be licensed. This standard is not difficult to meet. The State license may be obtained in cooperation with the agency.

WHERE ARE HOMES NEEDED?

War homes are needed within a fifty-mile radius of Cleveland. They may be either in the city or in the country. Often country homes prove especially valuable, but should be within reach of public transportation.

Homes somewhat outside a fifty-mile radius will be considered.

THE WORK OF THE BOARDING PARENT

The principal job of the families that decide to take care of war-home children is to look after these children from day to day as they would their own. The agency will help shoulder the major responsibilities and major decisions, such as those regarding school programs, special medical care, and the child's return to its own relatives.

Boarding parents are not liable for injuries received by the child unless their own negligence contributes to the accident. They are not liable for the damage done by the child to other people's property unless they take part in that damage or unless, having foreseen it, they failed to take steps necessary to prevent it.

HOW LONG THE CHILD WILL STAY

Some children need a boarding home for only a few months. Others will need help of this kind until they are old enough to strike out on their own. The length of their stay with boarding parents depends on the child's circumstances and need.

VISITS BY THE CHILD'S RELATIVES

Many of these children have relatives who may want to visit them occasionally. The agency arranges for these visits but always at the convenience of the foster parents. The same applies to visits by the child to the relatives.

TYPICAL WAR-HOME CHILDREN[1]

Marylin is not beautiful, but the sort of child one might want as one's very own. Her mother is dead and her father has just been drafted. Marylin is tremendously proud of her father. What is wanted is a home where Marylin can be made to feel at home, but where her loyalty and love for her father will be encouraged and not, however subtly, transferred to the boarding-home parents. This will call for real self-discipline on the part of the foster parents.

Johnny cannot tell anyone what he wants. He is only six weeks old. But a six-week-old needs the *personal* love and attention that no one, however devoted, can give to a whole nursery full of children.

[1] To save space, several of the case stories in the statement have been omitted.

143

Mary is frightened of the other children at the Detention Home, where she has been waiting three months for a home. It isn't that the other children are rough, but that Mary has been so much scared by the kind of life she had previously that she would be afraid of shadows. She needs the gentlest of handling in a small family group if she is ever to face the world four square again.

Three children have a father who is a merchant seaman —his only trade. Their mother is dead. The children were left with friends in the South. The father returned and found the children were not getting good care. He applied in the South for an institution but as his legal residence was Cleveland he was told to come here. He prefers a family life for the children. He will be back from voyages from time to time and wants access to his children. There are three girls, ages 7, 6, 4.

Child, 6, girl, is illegitimate. Placed by mother in institution. Has had good care there but now at 6 has never known normal family life, never had a mother. Is with children far younger than she—sleeps in a crib too small for her, as institution hasn't beds her size. Has had no stimulation to grow up. Has become unresponsive, frightened, suspicious of people outside the institution.

NOT A NEW NEED *BUT* INTENSIFIED

Many Cleveland children have been taken care of in boarding homes during past years. Indeed, one family of boarding parents has been caring for children for 25 years. There are now approximately 1,500 boarding homes caring for over 2,000 children in the Cleveland area. Thus Cleveland has had long experience with this type of care and has found it of immense benefit.

The situation now is that the circumstances which create broken homes have been much increased by the war. Simultaneously the ease of securing high-paying war jobs has tended to decrease the number of available boarding homes. It is clear, however, that caring for our children properly now, so as to assure them of a sound future, is quite as important to our country as manufacturing armaments to protect that future.

For further information, call War Homes for Children, Cherry 6850, or fill the coupon below.

WAR HOMES FOR CHILDREN

War Service Center, Public Square, Cleveland
I am interested in learning more about taking a child into my home.

Husband's Name.............................

Wife's Name..............................

Address.......................................

Protestant........Catholic........Jewish.......

Perhaps nothing in the casework field gets as wide a coverage as do campaigns for foster homes.[1] Combining the always moving appeal of the needs of children (for shelter and affection and intelligent care) with the appeal to the individual members of the public not to give but to *do* something, they are, in the current vernacular, "naturals." Especially as they lend themselves to illustration, whether by drawings and photographs[2] to accompany the printed word, or by dramatization for the radio; and by the swift appeal of the simple case story for almost any medium.

[1] See also Chapter VIII.

[2] Caseworkers usually oppose the use of photographs of clients for publicity. Many, however, see no harm in publishing photographs of small children, if necessary permissions are obtained.

Yet for all the publicity which such campaigns get, and though they publicize the services of which casework is the basis, they tell the public little about the casework involved in foster home-finding and in keeping in touch with the children, their own parents, and their foster parents, after the homes have been found.

The Cleveland campaign described above, like the others which we have had opportunity to study, omits this subject. To be sure, part of the casework task is implicit: the public can probably take for granted that to size up a foster home requires skill. But there is a wide difference between an investigation of the cleanliness, probity, and pleasantness of foster homes, and casework standards of studying both the homes and the children, and of working along with the foster parents after placement.

Even in this excellent Cleveland campaign, the public learns nothing about how the caseworker helps a potential foster mother to know just what her task would involve; how to know the special kind of mothering which a foster child, as distinguished from an own child or adopted child, should have; how to make the child feel loved and cherished, and yet not endanger its attachment to its own parents; how to co-operate with these own parents, so that they, too, can feel their child is not being weaned away from them, or that their responsibilities—though they may be temporarily diminished—are not removed; how to use what the placement agency offers in the way of support and guidance, and how to take what it gives in the way of supervision; how to feel content in the unusual position of co-operating in the care of a child with its own parents, and a placement agency.

146

The omission of an emphasis upon the casework in home-finding campaigns is unfortunate, not only because of a lost chance to let the public know what casework can do for the children, but because such a knowledge would probably increase the offers of good and suitable foster homes. A woman, willing to undertake the physical care of a child, may feel unable to cope with personality problems such as she sees even among her friends' children. Yet if she knew she could call upon a caseworker to help with such problems, it might make all the difference between a yes and a no. The casework phase of home-finding should be included not only in campaigns but in the even more important (because more sustained) day-by-day interpretation of the caseworker on the job. In this way the public could get some knowledge of the *content* of casework, and persons who needed it could learn that such a service existed, and how to find their way to it. And many others not ready to seek it out could be helped by the spreading of information to apply some of its principles in their own personal relationships.

The Information Center

The establishment of an information center from which anyone can learn where to find the service he needs is a great stimulus to good public relations. Cleveland's Welfare Federation recently set up a *telephone* referral service, *Personal Information Center*. It uses the name "Miss Wells" for the person answering the telephone. To publicize it the Federation issues a series of posters, a directory of services, and a small leaflet for mass distribution; and produces a weekly daytime radio program which dramatizes the problems of a family or a person who calls "Miss Wells" and is referred to the right agency. All these feature the sentence "For further information on agency services, call Miss Wells at SUperior 2900." A copy of the posters, leaflet, and directory, along with a letter and a reply postcard, went to the presidents of 1,500 business and industrial firms of Greater Cleveland. Within two weeks 246 companies had asked for 1,200 more posters, 75,000 leaflets, and 1,200 more directories. Within a month the Center had received 101 telephone calls, requesting information, which involved referrals to 76 agencies. Comparatively few of the inquiries were irrelevant. Most of them had to do with the various family and personal problems with which casework agencies typically deal.

HEALTH AND WELFARE INSTITUTES

Still another Welfare Federation project in public education is its annual Health and Welfare Institute managed by the Federation's Department of Public Relations and its Interpretation Committee. First held in 1943, it was sponsored by the Welfare Federation. In 1944 it was co-sponsored by 38 community agencies, and two years later by 75 countywide civic, educational, and labor groups. This one-day institute in its 11 morning, luncheon, and afternoon sessions in 1946 dealt with housing, employment, mental health, and family relationships—all problems which concern the field of casework.

Here was a channel for reaching the public in which casework specialists took part in panel discussions along with judges, teachers, ministers, and others about such questions as "Is the American family disintegrating?" and "How can marriage and divorce laws be improved?" This exchange of ideas took place before audiences which in turn had a chance to express themselves during the discussion period.

An article[1] describing the 1945 Institute told how it reached a large non-professional public:

The process of securing co-sponsors and delegates disseminates an immense amount of information by direct mail. . . . Letters go, first of all, to all organizations, then to all delegates, then to all executives and board members of agencies affiliated with the Welfare Federation. The result is a total mailing list in excess of 10,000.

At the same time a publicity campaign shares the responsibility of informing people about the Institute and its importance to the city. This program includes stories, not only in the metropolitan dailies, but also in the labor and Negro papers, as well as in small neighborhood papers. It includes, too, from four to six advance radio shows, supplemented by spot announcements in increasing number as the time of the Institute approaches.

Both the individual casework agency and the groups or councils of agencies now wish to develop to their greatest usefulness the various channels to public interest—the newspaper, the radio, the annual report, the bulletin or other publication, the meeting, the conference or institute, the committee, the speakers' pool, the organization of volunteers for interpretation. Most of these are used from time to time by

[1] Bryan, Jack Yeaman, "Capacity Crowd at Cleveland's Annual Health and Welfare Institute," in Public Welfare (American Public Welfare Association, Chicago, Ill.), October, 1945, p. 222.

the Cleveland agencies, working together through the Welfare Federation, or separately, and often with a high degree of skill.

Two or three of these channels we have discussed in some detail. Others we have hardly mentioned. The annual report, employed widely in the children's and family field as a major piece for public information, was used for that purpose in Cleveland at the time of our study only by the Family Service Association. Nor did the casework agencies there report any outstanding, sustained use of the radio, although there are two year-round weekly programs making frequent use of casework material. One—the "Ask Miss Wells" program—is put on each Saturday morning by the Welfare Federation. The other—"I Found a Story"— is produced by Cleveland advertising men volunteering as "Red Feather Minute Men." In the latter each man is assigned to a social agency and takes his turn telling a simple story of how the agency helped some person or family.

Cleveland casework agencies take full advantage of the newspaper, that wide and long avenue to public attention. Because of the high degree of co-operation between the agencies and the press in this city, we are giving a separate chapter to casework in the newspapers.

CHAPTER VII
CASEWORK IN THE NEWSPAPERS

Toward the newspaper, with its broad and varied public, the casework field has mixed feelings. Because everybody reads the papers, because they reach parts of the public inaccessible to agency-sponsored literature, and offer not only a wider service but prestige and importance, the casework agency is always eager for newspaper space.

This recognition of the value of news, favorable editorial comment, and even simple mention of the agency, is streaked with timidity, fear, and discomfiture: timidity because the average agency is still inexperienced in the use of the press; fear of finding a story about a client which in some way violates a confidence or discredits the client or the agency; and discomfiture—especially at times of money-raising appeals—because of frequent lack of concern for the pride and dignity of the "unfortunates" for whom aid is asked.

Caseworkers are still unsure of what they may reasonably expect of newspapers, and equally unsure of what newspapers may reasonably expect from them. Is the best they can get a casual "name" publicity? Is the best they can give an assortment of superficial items about their work? Or can they establish a sturdy give-and-take relationship with the press, so that, as their work develops, as illuminating matter reveals itself, they can talk it over with newspaper representatives, and consider together how it can be used?

NEW ATTITUDES

Time was, in the early depression years of public relief, when relations between the press and social work were bad. Newspapers frequently attacked not only the public relief agencies but also those private agencies now identified with casework, which, before the depression and well into it, had been the main source of financial help to families in need. Even now, with public responsibility for relief fairly generally accepted, family casework agencies are still often confused in the public mind with the relief-giving agencies.

But in recent years casework as something separate from relief has been emerging into its own professional stature. In the course of this development, it has been building friendlier relations with newspapers. The caseworkers' growing clarity about their function, their increased ability to give simple clearcut information about their work, and a realization of their need of public understanding have helped them in their still groping efforts to distill from their experience matter of general public interest.

All this has stimulated the hospitality of the press toward casework news. True, the news columns, with their categorical imperatives of *who, what, where, when,* and *why,* still tend to exclude even the best human interest material, shorn of names and addresses. But many newspapers have come to respect casework's equally categorical imperative: to protect the privacy of its clients. They are coming to recognize a wide potential reader-interest in the case-worker's approach to old and new human problems.

In Cleveland—as previous chapters have indicated—an active co-operation has been established between the whole field of social welfare and the city's newspapers. As one editor put it, "a friendly feeling exists between all Cleveland papers and social agencies, and between the people in Cleveland and social agencies. . . . People in general do not necessarily understand social work, but they think it is good and they're for it. That is not to say everybody likes social workers. Many think of them as a little apart from the human race. But I would say this: that everybody likes social work. The newspapers, naturally, reflect this feeling."

The social agencies and the newspapers both make specific efforts to increase the understanding between the two fields. Recently the Welfare Federation arranged a Newspaper Publicity Conference, so that social workers from all fields could discuss with Cleveland's editors, reporters, and columnists the best ways of getting publicity and interpretation into the papers.

Although the meeting was planned for the benefit of the social work field, the newspaper representatives found it of value to them, also. "We are here," said the chairman, associate editor of the Cleveland Press, "not only for your education but for ours. A new wave of interest on the part of newspapers concerning social work affairs has sprung up in this town." And later, "We can stand a lot of your thinking. . . . We are specialists in reaching the public. You must implement and guide us. . . . We consider ourselves as working with you. . . ."

It is not uncommon for Cleveland newspapers and social agencies—individually or through the Welfare Federation—to confer back and forth on matters of policy affecting community interests. One editor, for instance, asked the head of a family agency (among others) whether a certain judge would be a good person for his paper to sponsor as candidate for a court vacancy. Again, when the question of providing the best service to veterans was being considered, the Welfare Federation arranged a meeting between the military editors of the three papers and representatives of the various health, group, and casework agencies offering help to veterans.

CASEWORK IN THE NEWS

In all three of Cleveland's newspapers—the Cleveland Plain Dealer, a morning paper, and the Cleveland Press and the Cleveland News, afternoon papers—one finds frequent news of casework agencies and persons connected with them. And the words "casework" and "caseworker" appear casually, without explanation or quotation marks, as if on the assumption that readers will know what they mean.

This does not prove that the casework field has conveyed to the newspapers a real understanding of casework. Often it suggests only a taking-for-granted that casework is all right, a good and useful thing in the community, and that news about it will interest the readers.

When, for example, a new casework agency service is opened, an old one discarded, an agency name changed, a poll conducted, a crusade started to show some community need, a policy altered, a position taken in relation to pending legislation, statistics issued which show a trend related to some subject of general public interest—these things find their way into the news columns, often even into a good place on page one or on the first page of the second section. Sometimes they appear as straight news items. Again they are used as pegs for stories which advance the public's understanding of a service many readers might wish to use.

For instance, upon the opening of a Jewish Family Service Association district office in a middle and upper-income suburb, this news story appeared in the Plain Dealer of September 24, 1945:

HEIGHTS FAMILY SOCIAL WORK OFFICE
TO MAKE TEST OF AIDING MIDDLE CLASS

By Todd Simon

Carrying half-bushels of groceries up tenement stairs used to be the social worker's main job.

Now she untangles snarled home ties and snagged emotions. No more dole.

Quitting relief, family social workers also quit the slums. They found home troubles were as bad in middling and rich homes as they were among the poor.

Now, on Oct. 1, the first suburban family social work office here will be opened at Cedar and Lee Roads, Cleveland Heights. The Jewish Family Service Association will have this Heights office to offer help on domestic problems through schools and directly to homes.

When the social workers found that we did not have to be poor to have home problems they gave service to people who could and did pay for it.

Five Cleveland agencies accept fees for casework.

Miss Rae Carp, executive director of the Jewish Family Service Association, found that fee-paying clients acted differently.

Fee payers, even though they may be giving only $1 for an hour's consultation with their caseworker, show up on time. Many free clients do not. . . . Fee payers are more careful to use the full hour well . . . [they] respect the caseworker more when they pay for her trained help. . . .

"We have set no policy about fees for the Heights office," she said. "We base it on need and ability to pay. It's a nominal fee anyhow—one or two or three dollars for each hour.

"If they need the service and cannot pay, they'll get it free."

At the new office, at 2126 Lee Road, the caseworker will be Miss Lillian Greenberg. She has done consultant work for Cleveland Heights schools, when pupils' problems—such as moping, daydreaming, truancy or anxiety—have disclosed a troubled home.

She has also recruited a nonsectarian committee of Heights people as advisers for the new project. Veterans' groups, the Heights public health services, Cedar-Lee businessmen, parent-teacher groups, temple sisterhoods, school boards and block organizations are represented.

"Middle-class people always are left to deal with their health and welfare problems without society's help," Miss Carp said. . . .

"If their child gets tuberculosis, they can see that they owe it to society to report that and find ways to cure it. But what if the child is growing up to be a bad citizen? An ill-adjusted child is a danger and a burden to his society, too.

"They find it harder to accept help. But now we are coming to see that emotional sickness can be cured, often more easily with a trained person's help. And those with

156

problems will find that others in their social group are preventing or solving theirs by calling in a caseworker."

Miss Carp said two factors which helped her agency decide on the Heights office were these:

With employment and wages good, home problems did not decrease. In fact, the divorce rate grew until 65 per cent of court cases here were divorce actions.

And in the recent public opinion poll of the Welfare Federation three-fourths of Greater Cleveland women said they thought social work was for everyone—not just for the poor.

This story combines news with the kind of interpretation one associates with the special article. Often casework material and especially the problems of clients of casework agencies, though of wide intrinsic interest, are too chronic to have news-column value. When they get into the papers it is usually by way of the feature article, or the special column.

THE FEATURE ARTICLE

Take the following story, from the Cleveland Press of March 14, 1947, keyed to the news because the Youth Bureau was about to celebrate its thirtieth anniversary:

YOUTH BUREAU IS PRINCE
TO MODERN CINDERELLAS

By SHIRLEY KLOTH

Today's Cinderella with the cruel stepmother and the selfish stepsisters is exchanging her dream of a Prince Charming for the practical advice and help of a Youth Bureau social worker.

Typical of the adolescent boys and girls bringing their problems to the agency is 16-year-old Anne, whose mother died when she was a baby. Anne's father shifted her from one relative to another until he married a widow with two children of her own.

Anne hoped now she would have a real home, but soon came to resent the new mother who gave most of her attention to her own children. A clumsy, untidy girl, Anne drove away other people with her aggressive behavior, designed to attract the attention she wanted.

Anne was boy-crazy, and the boys who would go out with her took her to taverns, kept her out long after midnight. When she was home she sulked in her room.

She lost job after job, refused to obey her parents, and finally her father asked the Youth Bureau for help. When she came to the agency, she told the worker she expected a scolding, and that probably she would go to "reform school."

When she understood the agency wanted to find a home for her, she sobbed that she needed help, that she was just "a great big failure. All I want is to have my father all to myself, I hate everybody else."

But after a few weeks of interviews, Anne realized no one would like her if she followed her pattern of living. Before long she had a job, and had told the worker, "You're the nearest thing I've had to a mother. I can talk to you and you seem to understand."

Today Anne has a good job and is one of the many girls and boys who voluntarily are paying back the money the bureau loaned them.

"Our job is to give help and assurance to these young people who cannot find it in their own homes," said Mrs. Prudence Kwiecien, director of the Community Fund agency.

The two biggest problems the youngsters bring in, she finds, are how to work out a better relationship with their parents and how to make friends.

For 30 years Cleveland youngsters have been bringing problems to the Youth Bureau at 1001 Huron Rd. The agency will celebrate its anniversary next Tuesday with a luncheon at Hotel Statler.

A source of many special articles using the material of agencies in which casework is basic, is the need for foster homes for children. Child-care agencies are always searching for families who will give children affectionate, intelligent care for weeks or months or years, as each situation requires. They find many, but not nearly enough.

During the war this dearth could easily slant its way into the newspapers,[1] because the war had both created family troubles which plunged more children into the need for such temporary homes, and at the same time tempted many potential foster mothers into the war plants which were clamoring urgently for workers. And therefore many communities planned strong campaigns for foster homes and many newspapers lent themselves gladly to these campaigns.

All the Cleveland papers co-operated in finding foster homes. Our previous chapter showed how casework agencies, through the Welfare Federation, provided basic material for one campaign. Now we look at the way in which a newspaper used similar material in a campaign of its own.

The Cleveland News ran an especially noteworthy series of five articles, by Martha Lee, with the slogan "Homes for 100 Children by Christmas." They were written with warmth and accuracy. They made the reader see and feel the personalities of individual chil-

[1] See Chapter VI, pp. 137–147, for an account of the War Homes for Children campaign.

dren, and the specific and general situations from which the children had been rescued, and some of the difficulties in the tasks which prospective parents were being asked to undertake. To quote from one article:[1]

These children, awaiting placement, come directly from homes in which they knew filth, abuse, hunger, cold and poverty and the terror of being locked up alone. Many have had no home training. One child, who had never eaten at table or used silverware, dived into his plate of food like a puppy.

They are not all blonde, blue-eyed magazine cover children.[2] They do not all behave like angels. So they offer a real challenge to the foster mother and father who have faith in the miracles that kindness and good care can work.

Others have been in the Detention Home so long that they have temporarily taken on the characteristics of institution-reared children. These are fearful of new people, lacking in initiative, retarded in speech and skills, stolid and meek. But kindness snaps them out of it as quickly as sunshine revitalizes a droopy plant.

These articles also gave accurate information about the kinds of homes required, explained what the County Board of Child Welfare would pay for each child's board, and made it clear that the homes must be more than a place to stay, that they must provide affection and intelligent care. The writer, for instance,

[1] "Foster Parents Needed," in the Cleveland News, November 28 to December 2, 1944.

[2] It is interesting to compare this story with one which appeared in another city. Under the headline "Tiny Blonde Angels Seek a Home" it begins: "Anybody want three little blonde angels for Christmas? No, you don't have to write a letter to Santa Claus. Just step over to the Children's Society. If you're lucky, you may become the foster parents of three motherless children who could easily be mistaken for cherubs."

concludes one story of three small neglected children thus:

They'd like to feel they were wanted. They want to hear Mother Goose rhymes and take someone's hand and go for a walk. They want to say their prayers and be kissed goodnight, and sleep in a comfortable quiet room. They've never known these simple kindnesses.

Each of the articles concludes with some such comment. One tells of children waiting in the Detention Home "whose welts are healing, who are gradually losing their looks of terror" and who "need a real mother and father, and they'd like to find out what Christmas is in an honest-to-goodness home." And another: "She needs fruit juice, milk and hot cereal to fill out her thin cheeks, a full night's sleep instead of the catnaps wherever she can get them; and childish songs and fun instead of the beer-hall variety. She needs a foster mother and father who will treat her like a little girl."

This series of foster home articles is only one of several of Cleveland's child-care campaigns. The Emergency Child Care Committee, set up by the Welfare Federation, carried on a crusade not only for foster homes but also for Day Care Centers, and for Day Care for Children in Private Homes. All of them got good newspaper publicity, but especially the last, which grew out of an idea of a columnist then on the Cleveland Press, Mrs. Theodore Hall. Her appeal to private families to care for one or two children during the mothers' working hours, brought the offer of some 500 homes, two-thirds of which, upon investigation, rated well, and 200 of which were granted licenses.

The following editorial launched the Press's campaign:

CHILD-CARE PLAN TO AID
MOTHERS IN WAR WORK

The Press today announces a plan whereby mothers employed in war industries can place their small children in "child-care homes" during working hours.

It is a plan which will bring together these war-working mothers with home-staying mothers, many of whom belong to The Press Cradle Roll and Toddlers' Club. Mothers who have not enrolled their children in these groups are also invited to participate.

This new child-care plan was conceived by Mrs. Theodore Hall, The Press' child expert, who recognized the danger of improper supervision for small children as more and more mothers went into war work. . . .

Joint sponsors of Mrs. Hall's plan are The Press, the Cleveland Welfare Federation and the County Council for Civilian Defense. A Committee on Care of Children has opened offices at 1007 Huron Road.

Briefly, here is the plan:

If you can take one or two children—no more than two—into your home and care for them (you will be paid), fill out the coupon which appears with this story and mail it in.

A Welfare Federation investigator will see that your home conforms to the few simple standards required. Your name then will be listed with other "approved" child-care homes and these lists will appear at intervals in The Press.

War-working mothers who wish to place their children can then select the name of a family conveniently located. It will be up to the two mothers then to make the remaining arrangements.

Many working mothers have been placing their children in uncertified homes, because there has been nothing else for them to do, Mrs. Hall said, and therein lies a danger to the community.

Mrs. Hall's plan complies with state and city regulations. The state has delegated its authority of regulation to the Committee on Care of Children. In charge is Mrs. Jeannette Marsal. The committee has hired Mrs. Randall Ruhlman as investigator. Volunteers will help Mrs. Ruhlman investigate homes.

What are the "few simple standards"? Merely that the home be a happy one, a clean one, and that the woman of the house be capable of taking care of children.

The rate of pay will vary from 50 cents to $1 a day, depending upon the ages of the children and the number of hours of care.

One factor which will influence the rate of pay will be the mother's salary. If it is low, she naturally won't be able to pay as much as others may be able to.

The foster mother will be expected to provide the food for the child or children, unless a child requires a special diet or formula that runs into extra money.

By opening your home and offering your time to care for these children whose mothers have to work—

You will be serving your country by freeing another woman for war work—and women are needed urgently in industry.

You will be keeping up the standards of the community by helping to prevent increases in delinquency and disease.

You will be contributing to the happiness and welfare of the war-working mother and her child.

You will be able to earn a little money.

This attempt to bring together these homes and the mothers who wished to use them for their children at first seemed a simple matter: just hand a mother some approved addresses and let her make a choice. But it soon became clear that to find the right home for the right children of the right ages, the right nationality, the right religion, in the right neighborhood was a complicated challenge.

To handle these problems, as well as many subtle personality problems which came up, required the use of caseworkers. And their usefulness had to be indicated to hundreds of persons—the mothers, the foster day-mothers, and the newspaper public—who had never thought of social work except as something for poor people. And so the publicity for this campaign soon included such statements as this:

Every mother who wants help in making day care arrangements must come to the Emergency Child Care office. Since no two mothers have the same problems, the consultant can tell by talking to a mother what type of home is needed for her child. No time is wasted in looking for homes that suit if this procedure is followed.[1]

The needs of children for foster homes or for many other services are, unfortunately, not in themselves news. But campaigns to provide such care or the establishment of new means for filling a need become news, and Cleveland papers play them up generously.

THE ADVICE COLUMN

In Cleveland papers, too, one of the best departments in which to find well-informed, understanding reference to casework services is the advice column. Cleveland has three of these—Martha Lee's, in the News, Mrs. Maxwell's[2] and Helen Allyn MacDonald's

---

[1] The Cleveland Press, February 4, 1943.
[2] Now called "Heart and Home," and written by Betty Wenstrom.

in the Press. A number of other columnists occasionally use casework material. These columnists know the work of the various social agencies, and not only frequently refer their correspondents to the right sources of help, but often give some of the basic philosophy or background information which would lead their questioners to gather just what kind of help they might get.

Mrs. Maxwell, for example, writes to a wife who asks what to do about an alcoholic husband, "It is the opinion of caseworkers who have handled problems similar to this one that drunkenness is not the cause of the trouble, but rather a symptom of underlying personality difficulties. They look at the alcoholic as a person not as an alcoholic." Then, after further discussion, she refers the troubled wife to Alcoholics Anonymous, the Institute of Family Service,[1] or the Jewish Family Service Association, giving the addresses of all three.

Again, answering another wife, whose husband runs away whenever he loses a job, she writes, "He needs someone to help him locate the reason for his running away from a situation that appears intolerable to him. With tact and patience a third party could help. You could seek such assistance by consulting either the Institute of Family Service or the Jewish Family Service Association."

Often the advice column references to casework agencies are brief paragraphs. Again a whole column may be given to some special inquiry. Here are excerpts from one column headlined "Security Is

---

[1] Now Family Service Association.

More Than Food, Shelter," by Helen Allyn Mac-
Donald in the Cleveland Press:

"Could you," writes a correspondent, "write something . . . about what happens to the children in the
family when their fathers run around with other women?"

The story she relates is not new. . . . It's the same old
worn-out record of a father telling the mother he is in
love with a young girl at the war plant. . . . "The mother
tries hard not to break down in front of the children, but
she can't help it. They aren't old enough to know why she
is crying, but it must make an impression on them, isn't
that so?"

It is so. We hear child experts talk a great deal about the
child's need for security. The experts don't mean financial
security. They mean a nice, warm, comfortable feeling of
being wanted by a mother AND a father. They mean the
confidence that comes to a child when he knows that
mother and father are happy and all is well in the home.

When a parent gets into an extra-marital jam, and the
mother . . . feels the bottom has dropped out of her
world, she would do herself and her children a favor by
crying on a nice, impersonal shoulder.

All may seem to be lost, but she's probably so close to
the forest, she can't see the trees. She is probably one of
the great middle class who shies away from professional
help because it still thinks social agencies, such as the
Institute of Family Service, are strictly for the poor in
pocketbook, as well as in mind.

It might help her—and it certainly would help her
family—if she could get her troubles off her chest outside of
the home; if she would talk over the whole business with a
professional caseworker without having the children "lis-
tening in" while she cried over the phone to her best friend.

It isn't always the husband who is to blame. It isn't
always the tired mother. But it usually is the child who
takes the brunt of the clash. . . .

Troubles can't always be ironed out, even by professional caseworkers, but it's worth a try for the family's sake. When the wife changes her own attitude, it sometimes makes it possible for the husband to change his, too. That's a good start toward security for the children.

Again and again one finds the advice columnists informing their readers that casework is no longer something for poor people only. Take the following column entitled "Reader Appeals Difficult Problem to Martha Lee" in the Cleveland News:

"I am a well-educated woman, living in a good suburban neighborhood, and I write under a pen name because I want my identity protected.

"Whether you realize it or not, we people in comfortable circumstances also have problems. They aren't the exclusive domain of the unmarried mother, the wife of the alcoholic husband or the philandering wife.

"I need advice, which I cannot get from my doctor or lawyer because I see their families socially, and this matter is too intimate and not strictly in the scope of their professions. I wouldn't consult my relatives or friends, as this must not become gossip. What do you suggest? And without meaning to belittle you, I could not trust sending this story to a newspaper."   J. M.

All my mail is held in strict confidence. I am the only one who sees it and I destroy it after it is answered. I know that many problems are beyond my realm, and I am the first to suggest professional counseling in such cases.

There are three suitable private social agencies in Cleveland which can help you. They are the Institute of Family Service, the Jewish Family Service Association and Catholic Charities.

While we used to think of the social worker as someone who came around with a basket on Thanksgiving, you'll find that the trend has changed remarkably. The emphasis in the private agencies now is casework service, and the number of clients from the upper and middle income brackets is rapidly increasing. As you point out, no one economic group has a corner on personal problems. They invade the palace as well as the hut. You may consult these agencies on the same basis as you would a doctor or lawyer, paying for your service, and expecting and receiving confidential handling of your affairs.

Miss Anna B. Beattie, educational secretary of the Institute of Family Service,[1] tells me that only 12 per cent of their cases involve relief. Many of their clients pay a fee, from 50 cents up, according to their ability to pay. Sidney Berkowitz, casework supervisor of the Jewish Family Service Association, says only 10 to 15 per cent of their cases involve giving relief. Miss Florence Mason, assistant director of Catholic Charities, reports a similar trend in her agency.

It has taken the social agencies a long time to sell themselves to the public in this capacity, for we still tend to identify their clients as impoverished or unable to handle their own affairs. That stigma is fast disappearing, and I believe when people realize that professional advice is available and much more satisfactory than the opinion of the woman next door, they will consult them as readily as they will their doctor.

KEEPING OUT OF THE PAPERS

The friendliness and understanding between press and casework agencies show not only in what the papers print, but in what they do not print.

---

[1] Now Family Service Association.

Nearly every casework agency has suffered from an unfairly reported case story—the tale of a family evicted though under the care of a relief agency, or of a family to whom an agency has refused help or otherwise mistreated. Even now, once in a great while such a story slips into a Cleveland paper. But it is practically routine for all Cleveland papers to check with an agency about any client. For this purpose the papers keep on file both the day and night telephone numbers of representatives of the leading agencies.

It was eight-thirty one morning that a reporter called the casework supervisor of the County Child Welfare Board. An eighteen-year-old girl—who had been taken to a hospital because she had swallowed a handful of bobby pins—had jumped out of the hospital window and killed herself. The reporter, learning from the hospital record that the girl was legally a ward of the Board, was telephoning to ask for some background information, including the names and addresses of other members of the family. The case supervisor told of the girl's mother in one mental hospital, and of a brother in an institution for mentally disturbed children. She also told of a sixteen-year-old sister in high school who, unlike the others, seemed normal and was getting along fairly well. Then she pointed out the devastating effect which newspaper publicity might have upon this girl. The reporter understood. "Don't worry about the other papers either," he said. "I'll see the boys on the beat. We'll keep her out of it."

A Long Time Growing

The excellent relations between social agencies and the press have been a long time in the making in Cleveland. They began back in 1904, when James F. Jackson came to Cleveland as general secretary of the Associated Charities. He had a strong conviction that good public relations were of the essence of an agency's philosophy. "Through press, printed report and word of mouth," he said, "we must keep an intelligent, generous public informed of the needs of a rapidly growing city." But though he took steps from the start to let the press know of these needs, and though the papers co-operated with him in many ways, it was a long slow pull. He used to say that he read them every night "to see in what ways they have denounced me."

As late as 1921 and 1922 his agency and all the charitable agencies were fair game for press attack. The chief criticism then was that they did not help the poor promptly or generously enough. The Sunday Plain Dealer front-paged one particularly bad case under the headline "Children Beg Pennies in Snow Storm to Bury Dear Dead Rosella." On Monday the other papers took it up. Reporters besieged the district office which had known "dear dead Rosella's" family. There the caseworkers, disturbed at the misrepresentation and afraid of reporters, refused to give any information, insisting that their work was confidential.

This only increased the reporters' indignation—a needless complication. For as soon as the head of the agency presented the facts—that dear dead Rosella's mother had an insurance policy of several hundred dollars, two working sons and a boarder; and that, contrary to newspaper reports, the agency had never suggested that she sell her piano—the papers were convinced.

Two good things came of this bad incident: the city desk editors promised in the future to check facts with social agencies; and the Associated Charities established a policy as to how its caseworkers should deal with the press.

This policy did not spring into effect full blown. It grew out of a series of staff conferences about what could be told to newspapers, and how to tell it; what could not be told; and what to do when a story broke. It was based on the premise that, once they understood one another, social agencies and the press could work confidently together.

Although this active relation with newspapers began in the Associated Charities it quickly spread to the other agencies, partly because many of Cleveland's caseworkers had been trained or had worked in the Associated Charities, and partly because of the agencies' habit of pooling their experience.

Once in a while, as we have said, a story with unfair implications does slip through. Such instances call forth no recrimination, but rather some such approach as "If you're doing another story you might like to have these facts."

Working with Newspapers for Community Action

The mutual understanding between Cleveland newspapers and casework agencies makes it natural

for them to work together for community betterment. Out of long experience in helping people one by
one, the casework agency learns many of the weak
places in the social fabric. It knows that if people are
to be effectively helped, there must be community
interest and action. No amount of casework will solve
the torment of a family of an idiot child if the community fails to provide the child with kindly care in a
good institution. Nor can casework cure bad housing,
unemployment, typhoid, or any of a score of other
sources of human ills. But it can bring to bear—for
general public use—the knowledge heaped up in its
slow individual tasks. The forward looking casework
agency sees such use of its experience as an essential
duty.

This requires several basic skills: skill in seeing the
individual case in relation to large social issues; skill
in presenting casework in such a way as not to harm
any client; and skill in establishing good working relationships with the various agents of public opinion.

In Cleveland all these skills have been frequently
used, by individual agencies and groups of agencies
working together through the Welfare Federation,
and they have brought about a good many useful
social measures, and have pricked the public conscience to action toward securing other reforms.

A favorite channel through which to work for social
action is the press, and Cleveland caseworkers turn to
it as a matter of course, especially when numbers of
its clients are adversely affected by some community
fault.

A Family Service Association caseworker, for instance, found families living in slapped-together one-

room shacks and old chicken-coops in a newly opened area where anybody could buy a lot for ten dollars, put up four walls and a roof and a privy, dig a shallow well, and call it home.

The general secretary of this agency not only called these conditions to the attention of the County Health Commissioner, but gave an interview to a newspaper.

The ensuing publicity, which called the section a slum, stirred up protests from a better part of the neighborhood. The protesters, however, soon agreed that right use of publicity might bring them city water and a sewerage system; and they were grateful for the appointment with the newspaper editor which the agency head arranged for them.

In another case this director consulted a newspaper about Cleveland's Residence Law, which was hurting many families brought to Cleveland by war industries. Although some of them had lived in Cleveland several years, they could not become residents because they had "taken relief." This relief sometimes consisted in a single clinic treatment. In many instances it consisted in living in a housing project. (For a while children in housing projects had even been ruled out of public schools!) "A new residence law is needed," said Miss Helen Hanchette, the general secretary of the Family Service Association. "We cannot draft one ourselves, but part of our job is to needle others into getting the best people to draft one."

In this particular case the editor consulted advised that the moment was not right for newspaper pressure, but encouraged the agency to continue to collect data for later use.

A casework agency finds it comparatively simple to bring a general condition affecting many clients to the attention of the press. But to use a striking and dramatic case, which might be identified even if the papers agreed not to print the name, would give any good agency pause; for the confidential nature of an agency's relations with those it helps is paramount.

THE CASE OF HENRY

In one instance, however, the Cleveland Family Service Association decided to use such a case to blast at public indifference to the plight of Ohio's mentally ill and feeble-minded. The careful and humane way in which both the agency and the newspaper prepared and used the material is worth following in some detail.

The story concerned a ten-year-old idiot, whom the paper called Henry S. His mother's employer referred her to the Family Service Association when Mrs. S. had had to leave her skilled war-plant job, because she could no longer get anyone to care for Henry. She had tried for years to get some institution to take him, but though he had long since been probated and put on the urgent list, no vacancy could be found.

The caseworker who called on Mrs. S. found a despairing woman, who might have been doing urgently needed work, uselessly tethered to a helpless creature requiring constant care and watching, who could not make his wants known but could only babble, moan, or scream. She found also two high-school children, forced to seek whatever social life or recreation they could find outside, because they could not bring their friends into their home.

She knew at once that nothing short of institutional care for Henry would disentangle the family from its web of misery. And she knew that Henry was only one of hundreds of Cleveland's mentally defective or mentally ill children for whom the city and state provided no refuge.

There was no immediate, saving step the agency could take in this family's affair. But this situation, added to others like it, might be used to influence opinion.

To do this was a multiple task of interpretation, publicity, and public relations.

It meant a presentation of the case to the board; and discussing with the board the value of departing from its established policy of avoiding publicity about any client of the agency.

It meant getting Henry's mother's consent to publicity, on the grounds that it might ultimately help to bring about better care for Henry and for other children like him.

It meant getting a newspaper to crusade for such care.

The agency board voted that community pressure should be used. It decided to bombard the Governor, the Director of Public Welfare, the superintendent of the local institution and the Probate Court, with letters from the board members, from Henry's mother's former employer, and, if possible, from the Chamber of Commerce. (The board members wrote individual letters, deciding that these would be more telling than official board action.)

One board member suggested to the Cleveland Press a series of articles about problems stemming from neglect in developing state institutions.

The newspaper found the suggestion valid, and assigned a top-flight feature writer to the job.

This writer worked closely with the caseworker. They conferred on plans for selecting and presenting material. Not only Henry's case but several others were chosen. They secured authoritative statistical and other data about Ohio's treatment of the mentally defective and the mentally ill.

Then the reporter visited Eloise Hospital, in Detroit, Michigan—an outstanding state-county institution—to make a comparative study. She also went to Columbus for first-hand current information about Ohio's Institution for the Feeble-Minded there. Five excellent articles resulted. Three were published consecutively and two several months later.

Although individual families provided the impetus for these stories, the specific cases were used chiefly to illustrate a general condition. And not one article mentioned any client's name. Nor did the paper print a single picture of any member of any of the families described. The one photograph used—that of beds crowding a narrow corridor—was taken when the beds were empty. Thus the paper respected the right to privacy not only of the agency clients but of the people in the institution. No one reading the articles, however, needed photographs. The words provided the pictures. Take for instance the following from the Cleveland Press of July 13, 1943:

12 YEARS WITH IDIOT SON
—NO HELP FROM STATE

By Marion Hopwood

A bewildered, lonely woman will sit alone in her living room tonight, as she has sat days and nights before, prisoner of her idiot child who lies in an adjoining room.

She is bewildered because, although the state has places to take care of children like hers, her own efforts and the efforts of other responsible people have been useless in gaining his admission to one; and lonely because his presence has created conditions that virtually have driven the rest of the family out of the house and prevented friends from coming there.

For six years, since he was old enough to be considered, she has been trying to place the child in an institution; but for six years she has been told that there is no room for him.

If she got out of the house more she might happen some day to overhear another mother, holding a new baby close in her arms, say: "Oh, if you could only stay a baby always!"

And she would utter a shuddering protest. She has lived for 12 years with a boy who, due to a brain injury at birth, will stay a baby always. She knows what that means.

It means that he never has been able to learn to walk. Baby-like he lies in a special crib, with high sides to prevent him from rolling out, playing with brightly colored baby toys.

It means that he never has been able to learn to talk. He utters meaningless noises, low moans and sometimes heart-chilling screams that echo sharply through the little house.

It means that he never has been able to learn to feed himself. So three times a day he must be fed, propped up with pillows, with constant watch kept that his uncontrolled hands do not fling against the spoon, spilling its contents on him and the bed, or that grasping fingers do not happen on the plate and hurl its contents to the floor.

OFFICIALS ARE HORRIFIED

It means that he never has been able to learn any self-control. Like a baby, a dozen times a day he must be lifted out of his crib, his clothing changed and his bed made clean.

In return for this endless care there is no response of baby smiles, no affection—only the staring of vacant eyes and the tenacious grip of spider-like fingers.

Hardened as they must be by the problems of their clients, it is significant that even representatives of public agencies who have had contact with this family have been horrified by the conditions this child's presence has created in his home, and have tried to exert pressure to get him into an institution.

With no man in the family and the mother unable to leave the house to work, the family is on relief. Officials of the relief agency have tried to obtain care for the child but have succeeded only in getting him placed on the urgent list, where he has remained for three years.

MOTHER LOSES HOPE

Clergymen who have called at the house, visiting nurses, doctors, have tried to help, but without avail. And having been over the ground so many times, the mother watches their efforts without hope, although she appreciates the thought behind them.

It has been so long that she has lived with the care of her idiot child that she has given up hope that her life will ever be any other way. The problem of her two normal children is her greatest heartache. There is a boy, 17, and a girl, 15.

Fearfully she watches them spend more and more of their time away from home, on the streets, at movies or at the homes of friends she does not know. She is afraid for them, yet she knows that their home has nothing to offer them.

BODY IS NORMAL

She will confess that she has considered killing "the baby," or taking him to a public place and abandoning him

CASEWORK IN THE NEWSPAPERS

so that some public agency will have to take care of him. Then she apologizes shamefacedly for what she has said.

So, wearily, she goes about the physical care of her child. Wearily she lifts him out of his crib, wondering how much longer she can lift his heavy, normal 12-year-old body. Wearily she stands guard over him in the daytime and wearily she takes him into bed with her in the night and tries to quiet the screaming that keeps the other children from sleeping.

She has given up hope that society will recognize its responsibility and come to her aid. And even if it should, she is afraid that she and her children are beyond help. The mark that the last 12 years have put on them all is too heavy, she believes, to be erased now.

MORE OF THE SAME

Probate Court is starting on its newly revised records with more than 200 cases, as desperate and as hopeless as the one described here today. Some of these cases have been waiting for commitment to institutions for as long as 15 years.

Social workers might well regret the paragraph which assumes that representatives of public agencies must be "hardened," but they found the rest of the story accurate and telling.

Besides the newspaper articles, other pressures for social action grew out of the case of Henry.

The caseworker and the general secretary of the Family Service Association presented the case to a Welfare Federation group which had already been working for better facilities for the feeble-minded and for greater correlation of Cleveland's mental hygiene activities. This meeting "may have been one small

factor in hastening the organization of the Cleveland
Mental Hygiene Association."[1]

Then there was a meeting of 14 Ohio caseworkers
and executives attending a midwest institute. These
representatives of five cities, after hearing the factual
material gathered for the Cleveland newspaper articles, agreed to try to arouse their own local communities to the need for better care for the feeble-minded.
And two subsequent meetings brought reports of
progress in community concern.

An added gain was an interview in which an officer
of the Ohio Council on Family Social Work discussed
with the new Mental Hygiene Commissioner of Ohio
the needs as seen by family caseworkers.

What tangible advantages came of this publicizing
of the case of Henry? So far as Henry's family is concerned, things are unfortunately much as they were.
"The greatest thing accomplished," says the agency
account, "was the stirring up of public concern for the
care of those mentally ill or defective. Investigations
stemming from other quarters added their force to the
arousing of public opinion. The Governor appointed a
commission of capable people to study state needs and
make recommendations. Recently, a report from this
commission has been released and much emphasis has
been placed on need for more facilities and better
standards of care. One tangible improvement so far
has been the employment of a psychiatrist of excellent
reputation as State Mental Hygiene Commissioner,
so maybe in the long run the efforts on Henry's behalf

[1] Illustration of the Use of Case Material by a Case Worker to Interpret Community Needs, an unpublished report by Ruth Locher, Cleveland Family Service Association.

may bring results, if not to him—to others who will need similar help in the future."

The articles growing out of the case of Henry were published in 1943. Since that time all the papers have carried vigorous stories and editorials crusading for better care for the mentally handicapped. The earlier ones were chosen for detailed illustration here because they represent a specific, planned use of case material, a courageous departure from agency tradition, and an outstanding collaboration between a newspaper and a social agency.

We might also have reported on the late 1944 and early 1945 activity of all the Cleveland papers urging a good mental hospital program. This campaign, after persistent agitation, flared into a front-page flame when a feeble-minded fugitive from a state hospital killed a little girl. Investigation began. The papers reported lack of psychiatric examinations. One paper quoted a hospital superintendent who pled understaffing to explain his inability to prevent the escape of his charges. Another paper quoted staff members of other hospitals as reporting 78 "walk-aways." Editorials, private citizens, the court, Leagues of Women Voters, the Church Federation, all raised their voices, demanding better mental care. The Governor's Committee on Mental Health recommended a million dollar program. The papers cited the hundred million dollar state treasury surplus. Legislation began to get drafted, with the Bar Association sponsoring more bills. Wide legislative support was sought. Speed was urged—by special articles, editorials, news stories.

No one would claim that the Family Service Association's use of the case of Henry seeded this later outcropping of interest. Yet that original story stirred its own quota of passionate public concern, and the force of such widespread feeling will push ahead, long after its original impetus is lost.

Aside from what these articles did to arouse opinion about the care of the feeble-minded, they also did something for the stature of casework. The whole project was one more demonstration to the newspaper that a casework agency has a broader interest than the case; that it had the courage to depart from tradition; that it was willing and able not only to stimulate but to go along with a newspaper crusade.

The co-operation between newspapers and the casework field in Cleveland may be exceptional but it is not unique. In many communities over the country casework agencies consider newspapers their most useful medium of interpretation. And as this profession increasingly puts into practice its new philosophy —that of a service not for one unhappy segment of the population, but a service accessible to all—it will find the press, always sensitive to a wide reader-identification, correspondingly receptive.

CHAPTER VIII

ADVANCING CASEWORK'S FRONTIERS

C ASEWORK, which got its start in charity and its
greatest impetus in family and children's service
agencies, has advanced into new territory. Hospitals
and clinics, schools, industries, unions, institutions for
children, group-work agencies, the armed forces, rehabilitation camps, veterans' service agencies, even
an occasional housing project—all these in one community and another, employ some aspects of casework.

The use of this method of helping troubled persons
to find their way toward a working out of their
difficulties varies. It ranges from brief counseling
services—chiefly for the purpose of referral to suitable
community agencies—to sustained therapeutic treatment. Sometimes it is so thoroughly accepted as to
become an integral part of its setting—as, for instance, in medical social service, the oldest of the casework outposts. Again, it is undertaken almost as a
guest service, allowed to be useful as occasion arises—
as in some unions to which it has recently been introduced.

But however uneven its quantity and quality, or
the degree to which it is accepted, however fractional
in relation to casework as a whole, or to the need for
it in these new settings, some substance of casework
now reaches new thousands of persons. And its

philosophy is being found important in many kinds of human relations.

Wherever casework has broken new ground, this has come about by interpretation; someone saw a need for it, and gave tongue to that need until sponsorship for its fulfillment was found. Sometimes, as in medical social work, the impetus for the new service came from within the new setting. Again, as in Selective Service boards during the war, or veterans' services after, the use of casework was introduced by casework agencies or councils of agencies, often by the volunteering of services.

No matter what the genesis or setting of a new casework service, interpretation is a lifeline to its usefulness. Lacking the established casework agencies' momentum of long experience and community acceptance, the new service must strive harder than these both to create and to maintain interest, use, and support. Here, even more than in the family or children's agency, the caseworker finds public relations a function she cannot escape. For she works alone— or at best with only a few other caseworkers—in a setting where her work is only an auxiliary to the main preoccupations of the organization. She has to get her work understood, and valued. Perhaps nowhere is the quality of work more closely related to its interpretation than on these frontiers. If the work is not good, if the other members of the staff, board, or management do not see that it advances the primary purposes of their organization, it will not be supported.

In short, the outpost caseworker is a pioneer, with the double task of blazing new trails and keeping them open.

CASEWORK IN CHILDREN'S INSTITUTIONS

The extension of casework to children in institutions is an example of the pushing forward of a frontier from within the field of social work, with research and interpretation joining to accomplish this aim.

All over the country, there have for years been movements—backed by local study and by studies of the federal Children's Bureau—to provide casework service in children's institutions. Its growth in Cleveland has paralleled that in many other communities. In 1930 only one of the city's children's institutions employed a caseworker. Now 16 have such service, either within the institution or, in the case of the Catholic Charities Bureau, as a separate unit.

The study which initiated this movement in Cleveland began in 1920, with a question as to whether the city needed more institutional facilities for children. The findings showed that on the contrary large numbers of children then in dependency institutions would be better off elsewhere—either in specialized institutions or in foster homes. The need to find more suitable places resulted in the formation of the Cleveland Children's Bureau,[1] which centralized the casework for all non-sectarian institutions.

How the use of the casework method in institutions developed through various studies and scrutiny by committees is another story. The part of it which engages us here is the material of these studies, available for the interpretation of the needs of children to staffs, boards, and committees.

[1] The Children's Bureau was combined in 1942 with the Humane Society, and in 1945 the name was changed to Children's Services.

Such material differs from that used in undertakings like Cleveland's War Homes for Children campaign.[1] It is prepared not for a general public but as interpretation to and basis for action by specialized groups who have a sustained and sustaining responsibility for the support, administration, and growth of a service. These groups need a knowledge beyond that of the general public. They must know more of the why and the how of the service. They need this knowledge for every new step, every widening out of any part of it.

In Cleveland a committee of the Children's and Case Work Councils of the Welfare Federation provides an outstanding example of such information, in a report on casework in institutions for dependent children.[2]

This report deals mostly with such technical matters as intake, treatment, discharge, aftercare, use of case records, size of the caseload, and provision for professional staff development within the institution. Yet its points come through with such clarity that the boards, staffs, and committees for whom it is written can easily make the material their own, and can use it to arouse interest in others. The following introductory paragraphs, for instance, give the special audience what it needs to know and to feel before considering the report's technical content. This kind of inside knowledge also enables its readers to answer the questions of outsiders with confidence and conviction.

[1] See Chapter VI, 137–147.
[2] Case Work in Institutions for Dependent Children. June, 1945.

There are two main reasons for placement of a child outside his own home—either the family situation is such that the parents do not provide proper care for the child; or the child, because of his own disturbances, must be separated from his family, and there is usually interrelation between these reasons.

The institution is one treatment resource available for certain children who must be separated from their own families. It is a setting in which the child is helped through group living and individual treatment to be better prepared for his future. It is a means to an end and not an end within itself. It must be related to other placement resources in a well-integrated program. The length of placement in the institution depends upon the individual child's need, his family situation, and the availability of other community resources. It is recognized that the institution does not provide family life, and the value of the placement comes from the group living experience. It is paramount that the institution's program should be flexible to fit the child needing service, and not to fit the child to the institution.

The objective of the casework program within an institution is to implement individualization in the work with a child within the group setting; to determine when he should enter this setting and when he should leave it; to enable the child to make the best use of the services of the institution as well as to help strengthen the ability of the institution to understand and meet the needs of the individual child; and to be responsible for the relationship between the child and his parents as well as with the outside community. This latter implies service to the family throughout the placement period.

This simple introduction sends the reader on easily to the subject of intake. A chill, dim word, *intake*. But almost immediately it acquires meaning and warmth, for a listing of specific questions shows that it has to do, not primarily with problems of the institution or even of casework, but with the best way of considering each individual child:

Is it necessary to separate the child from his present environment or are there other ways of meeting the problem without resorting to separation?

If separation is necessary, what are the particular needs of the child and what specific placement resource can best meet these needs—i.e., relative's home, foster home, day care, institutional care, etc.?

If institutional care seems indicated, does the program of the institution where the intake study is being made meet the needs of the client better than other available institutional resources?

Again, a roster of types of children who would benefit from placement in a dependency institution, and of those who need other kinds of care, becomes in itself an interpretation. In the first category one finds:

The child who has such strong family ties that his acceptance of substitute parents would be difficult.

The child of separated parents who is being used as a pawn by them to meet their own needs. This situation is heightened when one or both of the parents have remarried.

The child of certain inadequate parents, who, because of their attitude toward failure as parents, seem to prevent another family's success with their child.

The child who is unable to form any close relationships with adults such as are required in a foster home.

The child who has had a succession of failures in foster homes and is in need of a less personal environment before again attempting family life.

The child who requires a period of close and continuous observation in order to determine his needs. The institution which cares for children in small units affords an opportunity for this.

The child needing regular habit training is more easily helped by the institution.

The child who needs protection from unstable parents.

And, among the types of children for whom "placement in the ordinary dependency institution is not beneficial," the report includes:

Infants, babies, and preschool children, the danger of group placement being proportionately greater for the younger child. Foster home care is preferable for preschool children. However, if in an emergency period group placement is necessary, a very specialized program should be provided.

Full orphans, who are in need of the security of substitute parents and family life.

Feeble-minded children and children with serious health afflictions such as epilepsy, cardiac involvements, diabetes, post-encephalitis, etc., all of whom need more specialized care.

The extremely hyperactive child, who is so overly stimulated by group living that further damage is done to himself as well as to the other children in the institution by his inclusion in the group.

The child who is already so completely withdrawn that he would be overwhelmed by group living.

All the above material, though technical in substance, is simply stated. So, too, is the following section entitled "Preparation of Parents, Child, and Institution for Placement Within the Specific Institution."

PREPARATION OF PARENTS

This includes full discussion of the reasons for placement; the meaning of separation to all members of the family; and help in handling this situation. They must be acquainted realistically with the institution and its program. It also calls for a clarification with the parents of what this placement may or may not accomplish and realization that this placement meets the present need but requires continuous re-evaluation. It is essential that the parents be helped . . . in making the placement a constructive experience. This means co-operating with the institution in such matters as financial responsibility, visiting plans, medical care, etc.

PREPARATION OF THE CHILD

The child must be helped to understand and to accept the necessity for this placement for him. He must be given an opportunity fully to express his feelings. . . . As with the parents, the child must be acquainted with all significant aspects of group living. He must be given some understanding of this placement as a plan that best meets his present needs.

PREPARATION OF THE INSTITUTION

The institution should be thoroughly prepared to make the child and parent feel accepted. This means the staff's knowing well in advance why this particular child is coming, where he comes from, what he is like, and what he needs. . . . Wherever possible, a visit to the institution should be arranged for the parents and the child previous to placement.

As the above quotations show, this report is *inside information* for staff and board use. Yet, because it states its facts clearly and because it always keeps the welfare of children sharply in focus, it becomes a basis and source for general interpretation. A good newspaper reporter or special article writer could find in it both casework information and philosophy, which is often groped for in vain; and groped for not only by writers, but by caseworkers themselves. It should serve to guide the caseworker in the selection of case stories and other illustrative material, to be given to the special writer, or to be used otherwise in publicity and interpretation. And the report loses none of its technical value—on the contrary, it gains value—from this wider usefulness.

CASEWORK IN INDUSTRY

The use of casework in industry came about in a different way from its use in children's institutions. Here the need for a method of helping people is felt less on behalf of those to be helped than by industry itself. Industrial plants everywhere have found that the various emotional quandaries of employes—home troubles as well as frictions and maladjustments on the job—increased absenteeism, labor turnover, and production costs. During the war the Federal Security Agency felt this to be so acute a problem that it appointed a special Counseling Committee of Community War Services to look into it. The Committee—made up of representatives of 14 government agencies and national private organizations— prepared a handbook for use by industries entitled A Guide for Establishment and Operation of In- Plant and Community Information and Counseling Services for Workers.

But for many years before this, various companies had been seeking ways to cope with the emotional and social troubles which were hazards not only to their employes but also to industry. In their search they worked out various kinds of counseling services. Some consisted of the hit-or-miss assignment of a supervisor or foreman with the knack of getting on with people to head a counseling staff. Others were based upon sound research, analogous to what the plant might conduct in other departments. (Perhaps the most outstanding of these last is the Western Electric Company's counseling plan, the fruit of a research project conducted in collaboration with Harvard University. In this study techniques for interviewing, not unlike some of those of casework, have been developed.)[1] Some plants found their way to the casework services available in the community, and built up techniques of referral to the various social agencies. This method had the double advantage of putting to use a wide range of resources, and of combating a frequent suspicion of employes that the plant counselors might be company investigators.

Cleveland industries have experimented with counseling for some time. During the war the problems, especially those affecting women employes, increased in number and in complications. An association of some 45 industrial personnel women from various plants, dissatisfied with their trial-and-error counseling, sent a representative to Western Reserve University. She explained that they were confronted with

[1] Roethlisberger, F. J. and Dickson, William J., Management and the Worker. Chapter XIII, The Interviewing Method. Harvard University Press, Cambridge, Mass., 1939.

all sorts of situations which they did not know how to handle. They thought there must be someone in Cleveland who knew more about human nature than they did and who could arrange a course of study for them. They would take responsibility for recruiting for it, and would help set up its plan.

As a result, Western Reserve's School of Applied Social Sciences selected Mrs. Olive K. Bannister, a member of its faculty, to give the first seminar provided by a school of social work for industrial personnel counselors. Sixty-one women, representing 13 plants, attended.

This course did not try to make caseworkers of its class members, but to let them learn—among other things—what casework is, in what situations it would be helpful, and where it could be found. And to select from its philosophy and its knowledge material of use to the counselor in her particular job.

Two comments of counselors attest its practical value. One said, "I've spent a lot of time and energy doing things for and with people in my plant which I was totally unequipped to do, and which the community had resources to handle far better than I could." Another commented, "I am glad to know their [the social agencies'] services are available not only for the people we work with, but for us, too."

This seminar for counselors was so successful that other courses have since been given.

CASEWORK IN UNIONS

In various communities unions use casework. Sometimes the service has been contributed by individual caseworkers, more often by casework agencies, or groups or councils of agencies. Perhaps the most extended use of casework is that of the National Maritime Union. It now has a social work staff of seven professional workers and nearly twice as many clerical workers, supported jointly by the Union and the United Seamen's Services.

In Cleveland in 1944 a few caseworkers, themselves members of the Social Service Employees Union, volunteered their services after office hours. A Committee of the Health and Safety Council of the CIO to Meet Wartime Needs sponsored them. Later, at the request of the Welfare Federation, three casework agencies each contributed the time of one caseworker for two days a week. Still later Cleveland's Welfare Federation employed a full-time caseworker on its staff to head the Workers' Service Bureau. This is a co-operative project of the Welfare Federation and the Cleveland Industrial Union Council of the CIO, representing some 100 local unions.

The caseworker pioneering in a union setting has to make progress slowly. Here, as with the industrial counselor, he must overcome some suspicion of being on the side of management. Also, common reluctances, such as the feeling that one should contrive to work out one's own problems, and that social agencies are only for poor people, seem heightened in this setting. He must interpret not only the services available, but the dignity in their use.

The first caseworker in the Cleveland Workers' Service Bureau, Robert M. Schmaltz, concerned himself at the outset with health problems, especially those arising from industrial disease. In the early stages he saw his job as simply to let the members who discussed their personal problems with him know about community services, and that people who staffed these services were trained to help them. Often he had to inform the union members that they had a *right* to use these services, which were paid for by contributions—including their own—to the community fund; or, in the case of a public agency, by taxes. At the outset he found the unions a little suspicious, but this soon changed, and when he went into the Army they asked the Welfare Federation for another caseworker.

For some time after this service began, only a few members brought their personal troubles to the caseworker—some 30 a month. Now more than twice that number—sometimes as many as 100—come each month, and helping them involves referrals to a wide range of community resources.

This growth in the unions' use of the caseworker came about not only through one person's telling another, but through planned publicity. Reports and speeches to the Cleveland Industrial Union Council and to local unions; the distribution of leaflets on workmen's compensation, legal aid, and marital problems; the plan for a bi-weekly distribution of other pamphlets on new topics; special leaflets addressed to particular plants, and distributed at the shop gates; special articles—some by leaders in the social work field—in the various union papers; all these have helped to spread a knowledge about casework facilities in Cleveland, and have stimulated not only consultations with the Workers' Service Bureau caseworker, but direct use of the agencies.

"A caseworker in a union set-up," reported Mr. Schmaltz, "has to learn many new ways. For one thing, he must discard all social work jargon. This is extremely difficult. I hadn't realized how much I used it till I began working with the unions." On the other hand, it was much simpler to get his ideas across to them than to interpret to the general community. "We don't get bogged down in telling *how* we work. We simply state what a problem is, and what we do toward solving it"—a technique of interpretation valuable in many instances of public relations.

The union caseworker also had to get used to the members' readiness to bring up personal problems in meetings, without benefit of privacy and leisure. Again, he had to deal with telephone calls from union officials and shop stewards in plants all over town, about problems of particular workers concerning which immediate advice was expected to be passed on second hand. These new pressures compelled a sort of nimbleness in casework skills and skills of interpretation to union members and to shop stewards. But many of the requests, both by their nature and their volume, presented insurmountable difficulties. The Workers' Service Bureau realized that it must carry on a wider program of education and must train counselors among its members.

To this end it set up an eight session course (beginning in September, 1946), which aimed to teach these counselors:

1. To refer fellow workers with out-plant problems (emergency relief, medical care, unemployment compensation, family advice) to the proper sources of help within the community.

2. To become familiar with the practices, procedures, and services of community agencies, both public and private.

3. To use this knowledge and experience as a basis for purposeful participation through board representation, planning groups, etc., to improve services in the community.

4. To give service to CIO members by carrying on the [counseling] job as an integral part of the local union organization and program.

The class discussion covered the following subjects: The Union Counseling Plan and Its Relation to Union Structure; the Counselor and the Workers' Service Bureau; Interviewing and Referral Techniques; Overview of Community Resources; Public Assistance; Industrial Health; Health Services; Social Security Benefits; Workmen's Compensation; Unemployment Compensation; Veterans' Problems and Services; Legal Assistance; Family, Youth and Children's Services; Neighborhood Councils. The course also included a field trip to the Cleveland State Hospital.

Fourteen industrial workers from eight local unions enrolled in the course and of these, 11 completed it and were graduated. Although the number of counselors trained in this first course was small, there was such a demand for additional union counselors that three more courses were arranged and 100 counselors were graduated. The Workers' Service Bureau regards union counseling as perhaps the most fruitful of its activities, both in its potentialities for the extension of services and in its value in interpretation.

The use of casework through the Workers' Service Bureau seems to be well established in Cleveland. The

Welfare Federation pays the caseworker's salary and provides secretarial help. The Cleveland Industrial Union Council provides office space and supplies.

MEDICAL SOCIAL SERVICE

As long ago as 1905 Dr. Richard C. Cabot of Massachusetts General Hospital introduced the social worker "as a definite factor in hospital and dispensary treatment."[1] By 1913 there were approximately a hundred social service departments in the United States.[2] But even before Dr. Cabot's work, Dr. Charles P. Emerson of Johns Hopkins University had recognized the relation of social and personal factors to the treatment of patients, and with the purpose of training doctors in social service, had arranged to have medical students of the University serve as volunteer visitors in the Charity Organization Society of Baltimore.

The long development of medical social service resembles that of other casework. It has been a growth from concern with economic and environmental factors to concern for the emotional and personality problems of patients. The early medical social worker sought chiefly information about home conditions of patients, and their ability to pay for medical care or to purchase the appliances and medicines needed in order to carry out doctors' instructions. Her task of reporting on these matters to doctors and clinics, and of referring families in need

---

[1] Cannon, Ida M., Social Work in Hospitals. Russell Sage Foundation, New York, rev. 1923, p. 14.
[2] Ibid., Preface, p. vii.

to relief agencies, was comparatively simple. Today, with a fuller appreciation of the interplay between illness and emotional pressures, with the patient's recovery depending on the way in which such interplay is mastered, the task of interpretation is more subtle and demanding. And not only to the doctors, but to the patients and their families. "Illness," says a medical caseworker,[1] "tends to affect not only the individual's independence and self-respect but his mode of living and even his emotional balance. Too, it may affect his role in his family and the regard his relatives and friends may have for him. If these pressures become too great for him, he may not wish to recover. They may prevent his convalescence."

Little has been reported about the ways in which the medical social worker interprets her work to hospital and clinic staffs. For the most part the interpretation has been that of demonstration of the value of the work itself, and by word of mouth. Sometimes the medical social worker presents reports at staff meetings. Often the interpretation is left to the individual caseworker in her day-by-day contact with doctors and nurses.

The story of the changes and problems in the interpretation of medical casework would make a chapter in itself. So, too, would the public relations of casework in many newer settings—those already discussed in this chapter, and others. The war, which aggravated countless old human problems and precipitated new ones, greatly accelerated its uses both in familiar places and on new frontiers.

[1] Madsen, Mary I., case consultant, Social Service Department, University Hospitals of Cleveland.

On all of these, the caseworker carries on not only her immediate casework tasks but also public relations. For she must fit herself and her work into an organization with customs, routines, and preoccupations of its own. She has to understand and accept the points of view and the interests of people in a background at first alien or strange to her—a public relations task often hard for caseworkers absorbed in their own professional problems. But in these settings, even more noticeably than in the family and children's agencies, public relations become an important part of the casework task itself.

Against such difficulties, the caseworker also finds advantages. She reaches new clients under conditions which remove from their attitude the bugaboo stigma of charity. She is continuously demonstrating the usefulness of casework for a wide range of human troubles to persons who had not before known of the existence of such service.

In every community the school is perhaps the most fertile of the new fields for casework. For this reason, and because Cleveland has made a good beginning in its cultivation, we select it for further consideration in our next chapter.

CHAPTER IX
CASEWORK IN THE SCHOOLS

THE EXTENSION of casework to the schools is a
natural development. Nowhere do the malign
pressures of disturbed family life send up their
signals more consistently than in the child's behavior
in school. Nowhere can the teacher discover a more
logical ally than in the caseworker. Yet only a small
fraction of the nation's schools employ school social
workers, and the use of casework as an everyday procedure for any troubled school child is still on a far
horizon.

In Cleveland, schools and casework agencies have
begun to work constructively together. At this writing, 34 Cleveland schools use caseworkers regularly
assigned to them by individual social agencies. And
as many more schools—which frequently call upon
agencies in special cases—have asked for casework
consultants. Unfortunately, a shortage of staff and
funds retards this extension.

The use of casework in the Cleveland schools is an
achievement of interpretation. It began slowly, a
caseworker here and there talking over some problem
with a principal or teacher. Gradually, as this sporadic
use proved effective, a few school principals, agency
boards, and the Welfare Federation took a hand in
the interpretation. Not only teachers and principals
but parents, too, they felt, and, in fact, the community in general ought to know of this resource

available to schools. One agency appointed a sub-committee of its Board Interpretation Committee to visit school superintendents. A representative of another agency talked with the Welfare Committee of the Teachers' Union. Principals and social workers spoke at parent-teacher association meetings. The agencies, separately and through special projects of the Welfare Federation, arranged to have case-workers give a certain amount of time to certain schools.

Most of the interpretation in schools was done by demonstration—a necessity, because of the dead weights of misconception, prejudice, and, worst of all, unfortunate experiences with poor social work or alienating attitudes of social workers in the past. One principal, now an enthusiastic proponent for case-work, told how reluctantly she came to it. "Years ago," she said, "I called an agency about a child who had been locked in a room for twelve days, only to be told 'that kind of case isn't the function of our agency.' Well, I called the police. I was through with social work. But one day a caseworker came to school to discuss a particular child. The kind of questions she asked and the *quality* of her interest in the child, and what she was able to accomplish by working with that one child's parents, changed my mind. It was good, discovering that *other people, social workers, were interested in the same problems which interested us!* I asked her about some of our other children, and she was always willing to have me refer their parents to her. Often she could get the parents to understand what was happening to their children, and to want to do something about it. It was wonderful what a difference it made. Of course, she couldn't get every child straightened out. But she did it often enough, so that a number of the teachers in my school began using her as a matter of course."

When, after the help of a caseworker, a nine-year-old dullard begins to do good work; when a battling nuisance of seven stops fighting and begins to make friends; when a child who has had almost daily epileptic seizures goes for a month without one; and another child stops having vomiting spells; when a child who used to fall asleep every morning begins to stay brightly awake; when these things happen in a single school, the interpretation problem is no longer to persuade the school to use the caseworker, but rather to guard against too great expectations from casework.

Good casework is often its own best interpreter, but not always. Often the kind of help useful in one situation is valueless in another. Interpretation must be accurate and continuing. An indiscriminate enthusiasm for casework can hamper the development of its use. Some teachers, who expect too much, too quickly, because of accounts of the accomplishments of casework, refer families with problems which have been developing for years. And when the caseworker cannot clear things up in a few weeks, they are "through with casework."

For the most part, however, when the interpretation has been temperate and accurate, the schools are willing to try it and do not expect miracles. One principal, who at first thought the caseworker wasted time on "trashy children who are hopeless, anyhow," consented to let his teachers work things out with a caseworker. The results have changed his attitude not only toward casework, but toward what he used to consider "trashiness" in children.

Many Cleveland teachers believe that the use of casework in the schools has had a wider effect than just helping the children exposed to it. In some instances, they report, it has affected their attitudes toward other children; and some of the ways of dealing with troubled children have proved extraordinarily effective with the rest of a class. Some teachers feel that in ways not yet formulated casework is making a contribution to the field of pedagogy itself.

"For example," one of them reported, "take our attitudes toward quiet, timid children who never make any trouble and do passably well in their studies. It wasn't until a caseworker came to talk over a child like that, that I realized he might be a greater problem to himself, if not to the school, than our trouble-makers. A good many teachers are only just realizing that the child who takes no part in the play of the others, and who doesn't make friends, should be a serious concern of the school, and needs special help in the school as well as outside."

Schools vary in the way they use the caseworker. "At first," said a principal, "we used to get impatient because she refused to go into the homes and tell parents what they must do. But in time we learned that the very fact that the caseworker was not armed with authority gave her special influence with parents. Now we tell parents that the caseworker has helped in other situations like theirs, and if they want to use her help, we offer to call up and make an appointment for them."

PROCEDURES

The common procedure in a school to which a case-worker is assigned is for her to spend a definite time each week discussing the children who need help with the principal and teachers. If they decide together that the trouble arises in the child's home and that casework might be useful, the school gets in touch with the parents and tells them about the casework agency. On the other hand, the consultation often reveals that problems may have arisen from some strain or stress in the school itself, and the school wishes to work it out by, say, a different room or grade placement, or by some other adjustment at school.

One school, after it had used a caseworker for some months, organized a group of mothers to study how the school, the social agency, and the parents could work most effectively for the benefit of the child. This served to stimulate the teachers to individualize children in the classroom; and, for the teachers, secured from the parents more active co-operation than they had had before. Another school, instead of having each teacher go over her cases individually with the caseworker, found it helpful to have a number of teachers in on the discussion, thus making a sort of clinic of it. Another school reports frequently at parent-teacher association meetings on the use it makes of casework. As a result mothers have brought problems not only of their children in school but of their younger children, too, to the office of the case-worker.

The caseworkers vary in their way of working with schools. Some of them take an active interest in school affairs, attending graduation exercises, school games, and entertainments. "Our students," said a high-school principal, "speak proudly of the caseworker as 'our social worker.' They think of her as part of the school."

In another high school a Young Women's Christian Association volunteer in charge of Girl Reserves asked one of the casework agencies, the Family Service Association, to provide dolls which the girls might dress, and which then might be given to children in families being helped by the agency. This provided a good occasion for interpretation. A volunteer shopped for the hard-to-find dolls; the school made a contest out of the doll-dressing, and asked the caseworker who had been working with that school to talk about the work of the Family Service Association, and to tell some ways in which the dolls were to be used. She explained the value of having some of the dolls in the various district office playrooms, where mothers may leave their children while they have their interviews with the caseworker; or as gifts to children who for some reason need special attention, perhaps when a mother must go to a hospital for a new baby; or sometimes as a gift to a child for whom a new home must be found and who would find it comforting to have something she is used to and has loved, to take along with her. The caseworker who made the speech illustrated it with carefully selected case stories. From this experience the pupils got some accurate information about casework, and a satisfaction more interesting and more valuable than the vague sentimental glow they might have had from just "doing something for poor children."

Hindrances to School Use of Casework

The school staffs in Cleveland are by no means unanimous in their approval of casework. Teachers share with the rest of the population a good many misconceptions about social work. One of the most obstructive, here as elsewhere, is the notion that social work is for poor people only. Another—a remnant of the depression—is that the social worker's job is to investigate and discover if people really need help, and then to dole out an allowance inadequate to meet that need. Many teachers, during the depression, fined themselves a percentage of their salaries to supply certain needs not covered by relief allowances. They heard many stories of relief investigators, most of them bad, for people were less likely to talk much about good experiences. It was inevitable that the teacher—like the relief recipients—should confuse the investigator with the caseworker. (Indeed, many investigators were social workers, and most of those who had had no professional training called themselves social workers.)

It is not only a misconception of the caseworker's function, but the attitude of teachers toward their own responsibilities, which often make their acceptance of casework slow and grudging. Many teachers still feel that to call in a caseworker is an admission of failure to do something they themselves should be able to do. In one school, a caseworker reports, the teachers had worked out a sort of quota acceptance: it was all right to refer four children in a class, but "if you need help with more than that there's something wrong with you." In contrast, another school reported that many of its teachers found it a great relief to know that they could not be expected to cope with all the troublesome problems themselves, or to leave them in the hands of helpless or blundering parents.

ADVANCES IN UNDERSTANDING

The war made it easier for teachers to relinquish the idea that social agencies existed only to relieve financial need. "Eight years ago," said one principal, "900 children in this school were on relief. When we last counted, only 27 children in 19 families were on relief.[1] But though nearly all of them are now self-supporting, we are finding more and more families with problems to refer to a caseworker." And she quoted case after case where the war had twisted the lives of families of school children, and told how, in many instances, the caseworker had helped. Situations unusual before the war became commonplace: a small frightened child, left alone all night while his mother worked on the graveyard shift; children who had to wake themselves up, and get themselves dressed and breakfasted in time for school and, unable to make it, failed to go to school at all; children getting into mischief because, rather than go home to an empty house after school, they found it easier and pleasanter to do something with the gang, and to fill up an inner emotional emptiness with wayward conduct.

[1] This statement was made shortly before the end of the war. No later count has been taken. With many families now receiving unemployment and other social security benefits and strike benefits, it would be difficult to get a comparable figure.

Situations like these are not new. The war only multiplied them and smoked them out of the dark corners of poverty into new settings. It also made it easier to publicize them, and what the caseworker could and could not do about them.

It is more difficult to engage public interest for the child whose troubles do not fall into big familiar categories—the dull, inattentive child, who may be suffering anything from a lack of vitamins or a lack of affection, to the complications brought on by a low intelligence quotient. Or the temperamental or nervous, anxious child torn by jealousies or divided loyalties or strife in a disturbed home. Or the apparently incorrigible child, a nuisance to himself and everyone else. Each case different from the last. Each needing something special from the school and from the caseworker. Yet all having certain—or perhaps we must say uncertain—common denominators, which the school and the social worker must learn to discover, and then to use for a wider benefit.

The troubles of one such child provided a basis for the following news story in the Cleveland Press of December 11, 1945.

SOCIAL PROJECT EASES
PUPIL-PARENT PROBLEMS

By Marie Daerr

"Praise the Lord. You're not going to take my Jimmy away."

The mother of a Case-Woodland school pupil surprised Principal Libbie E. Yirava with this remark recently. A southern migrant, illiterate, who until only a short while ago felt only fear and resentment toward big city officials, Jimmy's mother has discovered that teachers and social workers are good friends to her and her child.

For almost two years the staffs of seven Cleveland public schools and Family Service Association workers have been co-operating to solve pupil-parent problems in the Central Area. Their project, still in the experimental stage, rose from an SOS from the schools to the Welfare Federation. It is operated by the Central Area Schools Service Committee and is sponsored by the Federation and the Cleveland School Board.

Participating in this project are Kennard Junior High and Rutherford B. Hayes, Case-Woodland, Outhwaite, Wooldridge, Dike and Glastone schools. Once every three weeks a case worker from the Family Service Association spends a half day at each school to help a youngster who, if ignored, might become a delinquent. She comes more often, if needed.

"The case of Jimmy and his mother illustrates a common problem—that of the migrant who doesn't know our ways," explained Miss Yirava, Schools Service Committee chairman.

"Jimmy's mother at first was suspicious of our 'prying' and convinced that we were going to take Jimmy away from her. She was finally made to realize that Jimmy would profit from more sympathy and less censure and that daily attendance at school was imperative.

"The project is new, but already has produced encouraging results," said Miss Yirava. "Johnny, who used to be habitually absent, now comes to school even when ill and asks to be excused. Bill, who annoyed the entire room with his antics, improved when his grandmother, a stern woman, was convinced that kindness was preferable to a slap."

On Miss Yirava's committee were the principals of the other participating schools; representatives of Sterling and Barnett Offices of the Family Service Association; Dr.

David J. Wiens, Cleveland School Board attendance chief; Frank J. Skelly, the board's Juvenile Court representative; and Miss Lucile A. Nolan, assistant supervisor of school nurses.

It is cheering that the picture which illustrated this story presented not Jimmy—whose privacy was respected—but the school principal and the caseworker.

A Committee of Teachers and Caseworkers

One well-planned step toward wider use of casework, as well as toward the spread of the use of casework in individual schools, has been made. Early in 1944, a school principal, a member of the Board of Education, and two caseworkers, formed a committee under the auspices of the local branch of the American Association of Social Workers. They planned a meeting to which they invited the teachers and social workers in one neighborhood—the West Side area. They expected only about 25. Instead, 75, about equally divided between the two professions, attended. At this gathering a school principal spoke on what the school teacher expects of the social worker, and a social worker discussed what the social worker expects of the teacher. The meeting aroused so much interest that the committee decided to have others, with smaller groups, in different parts of the city. During the next school year this special West Side group held seven such meetings, sometimes in schools, sometimes in the offices of social agencies—the Family Service Association, the Aid to Dependent Children, the Youth Bureau, the Children's Service Bureau, the Detention Home, the Juvenile Court

Building, and others. The group formulated its aims as follows:[1]

1. To get to know each other as individuals and to know the attitudes and philosophies of the two professional groups, teachers and caseworkers, in regard to handling problem children.

2. To supply an understandable interpretation to every teacher and principal in our area of what a trained caseworker is, what it is she tries to do, and what some of the techniques of treatment used by the caseworker are in individual cases.

3. To interpret to teachers and principals what caseworkers need from the school in the way of specific knowledge, and what is done with this information after it is obtained.

4. To keep individual teachers informed and to help them see what a vital role they play in the lives of the children whom they teach and how this influence can be used to help and strengthen the child as well as offer him satisfactions not found elsewhere in his life.

5. To acquaint social agencies with the areas in which schools need help as well as to have them understand where they [the social agencies] were found wanting in the past.

6. To offer an opportunity to teachers and principals to understand the function of the various casework agencies in Cleveland, through meeting representatives of these agencies and discussing cases with them.

7. As a group, to get so well acquainted ourselves with the above factors that we can plan a program of interpretation to other schools and agencies in our area, which will create a more understanding, better functioning relationship between the two groups.

[1] From minutes of the Teacher-Social Worker Committee meeting, April 2, 1945.

212

The subjects discussed at these meetings covered a wide range: the difficulties of teachers of large classes in sorting out the children with problems, and knowing to which agencies their parents should be referred; the problems of the caseworkers in explaining why behavior patterns in the making for years cannot be solved overnight; the ways in which the caseworkers helped the parents; and how the school could help one child in one way, and one in another; and how different social agencies could help different families. The caseworker had much to learn about the pressures under which teachers must work. The teachers had to learn what casework might and might not accomplish, and how the child's life at home and his relation to his parents and brothers and sisters and their relation to one another affected him.

At the first three meetings speakers discussed abstract principles and general practices. But presently the groups found it more profitable to give the meetings over to discussions of individual cases.

All was not sweetness and light at these meetings. Many complaints against social work came up, ranging from "the futility of referring cases to social agencies," "the slight hope of getting anything accomplished," "the slow pace of casework," to the accusation that "caseworkers looked down their noses at teachers." Despite these, or perhaps because of their being brought out into the open, the committee wished to continue the meetings. And another group, on the East Side, was started.

At the end of the school year, a spokesman for the teachers and one for the social workers summed up their conclusions. Because they show clearly not only the accomplishments and limitations of an unusual project in interpretation, but also some of the basic problems in the use of casework in schools, we are quoting them in full.

RÉSUMÉ OF MEETINGS OF WEST SIDE SCHOOL TEACHERS AND SOCIAL WORKERS FOR SCHOOL YEAR 1944–1945

Conclusions of the Casework Chairman

1. School teachers and caseworkers start off with an essential difference in attitude toward a problem child. The school seeks to reform him or have him be conforming in school. They see discipline as a means to this end. The caseworker never considers punishment as a solution but tries to understand the *underlying* causes for the symptoms. When these causes are corrected, the problem is helped or ceases to exist.

2. The school seems to feel that caseworkers can be used in the same sense as policewomen or at least as higher sources of authority and ability to "take action" than the school. This is a mistake, because essentially it is the function of casework to *study* and *treat* behavior problems. This almost always excludes the use of authority. Placement in foster homes or in disciplinary institutions is seldom used, and then *only* when any other solution is impossible.

3. As our committee has felt its way along, we have felt the only solution to a real understanding between our two groups lies in a slow, careful discussion of realistic problems we have shared, like the study of Thomas (a child whose behavior and problems the committee discussed in great detail). We learned through our earlier meetings that we did not learn significant facts by being told that they were so. It was necessary to understand their operation in an actual case which we knew. Because of this, we question how valuable any program of interpretation can be which

does not evolve through the same, slow process which this committee has experienced.

4. The casework group has felt that the caseworkers brought more interest to the project than the teaching group, who were frequently absent. The slowness with which the committee developed may account somewhat for this.

Conclusions of the School Chairman

1. I agree with the casework chairman that teachers and social workers have an essentially different attitude toward a problem child, and rightly so. For the most part time and energy limit the teacher's effort to students who conform to a reasonable degree, while the social worker deals with those who have unusual home conditions, or abnormal behavior patterns. A teacher certainly wouldn't attempt to treat a child broken out with a rash, she would send him immediately to the school doctor or nurse. In the same manner, when a boy or girl exhibits abnormal behavior a teacher generally considers treatment outside her province, and refers the student to the office. Teachers for the most part are long suffering and endure countless minor behavior infractions, or attempt various home remedies, generally disciplinary in character. Many times such simple remedies work, but there are always the obstinate cases that need special treatment.

2. It is only within recent years that the idea of mental illness has been accepted, its causes studied, and remedies suggested. The physical life of a child is much better known and charted, than the mental and emotional life. We are only just beginning to recognize the great need for guidance and understanding in this particular field. Teacher-training programs are beginning to include courses in Mental Hygiene. Such courses should cause teachers to be more sympathetic toward students who do not conform, and

enable them to identify behavior symptoms that need to be referred to a specialist.

3. Schools are often slow in calling in the social worker, and many times critical of results accomplished. This is due to lack of appreciation on the part of teachers and administrators of the fact that present behavior on the part of a student is due to causes of long standing and cannot be changed overnight. Most teachers want immediate relief, and not lengthy explanations. To be told that each individual case is different, and needs a long period of time for study, is of little assistance to a harassed teacher. Much of the present misunderstanding could be eliminated if a course in Mental Hygiene were to be required of all teachers before being certified. For teachers already certified to undertake this study voluntarily is perhaps too much to expect. Learning the causes should help a teacher to be more sympathetic, and more appreciative of any behavior improvements.

4. All during the year the casework group of the Committee has felt that the Teacher Group has not manifested sufficient interest in the Committee. Such a criticism may not be entirely justified. At present many teachers feel that the study of behavior problems is something outside their field, and that by the same token a social worker might be expected to teach a class at least once a month in order to appreciate the problems of a classroom teacher. Then, too, as teachers are an older and better established group than social workers they may not feel it necessary to interpret their position to any other group. However, as a representative of the teaching group who has attended the meetings of the Committee since its inception I feel amply repaid for any time or energy spent, and would like to make the following recommendations:

 1. That the size of the Committee be increased so that when absences occur there will still be a fair representation.

2. That another effort be made to have more schools in the area represented.
3. That administrators and guidance counselors be particularly urged to attend.
4. That parochial schools be represented.
5. That the Attendance Department be represented.
6. That the School Nurses be represented.
7. That the School Doctors be represented.
8. That every effort be made to interpret the total personality of any case studied by the Committee.
9. That all members of the Committee do their utmost to spread the findings of the Committee in the groups in which they are individually associated.
10. That acceptable personal, emotional and social adjustment be stressed as one of the primary aims of education.

It is heartening that a committee of teachers and caseworkers should have come into being, and, despite some snags and difficulties, should vote to continue its work. It is heartening, too, that 34 schools in Cleveland maintain a close and continuing cooperation with casework, and that teachers are recommending the employment of caseworkers—or "school social workers" as they are more generally called—by boards of education, and mental hygiene as a part of every teacher's training.

A Long Way Still to Go

But it would be premature to say that casework has found a firm foothold in the educational system of Cleveland. As with other kinds of social work—the health services, the various neighborhood settlements, community centers, and other group-work projects—

the school's use of caseworkers varies. Not every teacher, even in the 34 schools which use casework consultants regularly, takes advantage of them. And although many other schools ask for casework services for special children and want more such services than the social agencies can now supply, nothing like the full use envisaged by the casework field is imminent.

Use of casework will continue to increase in schools as each child helped demonstrates its effectiveness and as each teacher finds it furthers her task of education. There is, however, still a long way to go before teachers and parents see casework as something more than a one-by-one way of helping people; before not only individual schools but boards of education find it of value and employ, as part of the school system, an adequate staff of school social workers; and before the field of casework with the help of the field of education can evolve from its practices the basic knowledge which can be put at the disposal of a wider public.

CHAPTER X

THE TASK AHEAD

THE HEAD of one of today's leading casework agencies recently described her first day in social work about forty years ago in a private charity agency. For training, she was to observe the executive help the poor.

A woman came in with a baby.

"Sit down, my good woman," said the executive kindly. "What is your trouble?"

"We have no food in the house. My husband is dead. I don't know what to do."

"That's too bad. How many children have you?"

"Five."

The executive let her talk a little about her troubles, asking a question now and then. After a while she opened a drawer, and took out five dollars.

"Here you are, my good woman."

The "good woman" left. The executive entered the date, name, and address in a ledger, and under them "five children, five dollars."

It is a far cry from the groping benevolence of that agency of that day to the underlying philosophy and practices of today's best casework. Such progress, within the experience of many persons who are now leaders in social welfare, should reassure a profession which, rightly, sees today's accomplishments as a far cry from its envisaged goals.

The growth already achieved came from various roots: new and more liberal concepts of social philosophy; new knowledge gained in other fields, notably psychiatry; the long cumulative first-hand experience in helping people; the ability to tell others about that experience; and the development of professional training. Future growth will depend upon the same factors.

Of all of these, the telling is far the weakest. Caseworkers, intent on increasing technical skills in helping people, have given much less thought to establishing a strong sense of partnership with the public. Only thirteen casework agencies in the country employ public relations specialists. In most instances the executive tucks into an already overcrowded job whatever formal interpretation he can find time and skill to do. The individual caseworker gets little training or guidance for her own responsibilities in public relations—although she is expected to carry such responsibilities. Indeed they are forced upon her, in the ordinary course of her days, not only in her various on-the-job contacts, but in her outside social life.

The caseworker has had training in understanding and establishing a rapport with clients but not with the public. Our study of the public relations of casework in Cleveland shows that the individual caseworker tends to be rather afraid of the public. Her first approach—as the experiments with conversations reveal—is likely to be defensive, on the assumption that people will be, if not unfriendly, at best indifferent to or unable to comprehend what she might have to tell about her work.

But these same trial-and-error conversations showed how, with planning and experiment, the caseworker could greatly increase her skill in interpretation. They showed, too, that people were much readier with interest and understanding than she had expected. This public friendliness was brought out also by other experiments in Cleveland. The Welfare Federation's poll of opinion about social work, which included casework, showed that only 3 per cent of 700 women questioned disliked or mistrusted it. And as for the caseworker's assumption that people would find casework hard to understand, the children's answers to a questionnaire indicated that even children take for granted the need for it, and that it requires special qualities and abilities.

A study of Cleveland's three newspapers showed that the press considers information from the casework agencies to be of interest to newspaper readers, whether as news or material for special writers, columnists, and editorials. And the spreading use of casework services in schools, unions, group-work agencies, and veterans' services, for instance, showed that more and more the usefulness of and need for casework are being recognized.

We have seen, too, that Cleveland's outstanding casework public relations are not the result of chance, but are the fruit of many years of attention and nurture. Long ago the Associated Charities (now the Family Service Association) began to consider the spreading of information about its way of helping people an integral part of its work, and some responsibility for it a part of every caseworker's job. (As early as 1917 its annual reports emphasized the importance of "personal service" as distinguished from "material relief.") This agency was one of the first in the country to assign the full time of a special person to interpretation and publicity. Other Cleveland casework agencies, too, though they did not employ specialists for the purpose, took steps toward keeping the community informed and developed skill in various phases of interpretation. The agencies worked, both individually and together, through committees and through the Welfare Federation, to increase public understanding of casework.

Cleveland, though outstanding, is not unique in having established many good relations for casework. And its caseworkers would be the first to say that they are only at the beginning of what they hope to achieve in the way of public understanding.

To make casework better known, better used, and better supported—and indeed to make it better—is only one part of the task of public relations which lies ahead; and perhaps the least difficult part, for as this Cleveland study has shown, and as other communities can also show, excellent beginnings have been made.

More challenging is the task of distilling from the everyday experience of casework practice its wisdom about human nature and human relations, and putting these at the service of the public. True, individual agencies, local and national, have begun—in pamphlets and in talks to special groups—to carry on education for marriage and family life. And yet, compared to the widespread need for such knowledge, casework has done only a little. The most marked advances have been made in the children's field. Here writers who popularize information on how to bring up children frequently draw upon the experience and knowledge gathered by the children's services. But casework's experience in the field of adult relationships—though it has much to offer that is nowhere else available—is only beginning to be tapped.

To sift out casework's special knowledge of human relations will require time and money, search and research. And to make it widely available will require the development and the employment of skills in increasing public information, both among caseworkers on agency staffs and among specialists in the public relations field.

When casework takes its first long stride in this direction, it will begin to make a contribution to the field of human relations analogous to that which medicine has made to the field of public health. It will have stepped over a threshold into its own new era.

APPENDICES

APPENDIX A

POLL OF PUBLIC OPINION
regarding
HEALTH AND SOCIAL SERVICE
Welfare Federation of Cleveland

QUESTIONNAIRE

1. Do you think we will have a depression after the war?
   None_____ Moderate_____ Serious_____

2. Taking everything into consideration, do you think that people are better off_____or worse off_____ today than they were before the war?

3. Do you think family problems have increased because of the war?_____ Why?_____

4. If a serviceman's wife is having trouble with her family affairs, where do you think she should go for help?

5. Suppose you know an unmarried girl who is going to have a baby. Where, outside her family, would you suggest that she go for help?

6. Suppose you had a serious personal or family problem. To whom would you go for help?

7. Suppose you know a couple whose quarreling is so serious that it is affecting their children. Where do you

---
[1] Discussed in Chapter V.

227

think they could get help? (Number according to order of choice.)

a. Doctor
b. Lawyer
c. Newspaper columnist
d. Policeman
e. Social worker
f. Political leader or councilman

g. Court
h. Pastor
i. Psychiatrist
j. Mr. Anthony
k. Welfare Federation
l. Other:
m. Don't know

Reason for first choice:

8. Suppose you were the parent of a 14-year-old boy or girl who was running wild and getting out of your control. From which of the following would you seek help? (Number according to order of choice.)

a. Juvenile court
b. Newspaper columnist
c. Institute of Family Service
d. Settlement house
e. Mr. Anthony
f. School principal
g. Youth Bureau
h. Girl Scouts or Boy Scouts
i. Pastor

j. Social worker
k. Policeman
l. Welfare Federation
m. Political leader or councilman
n. Cleveland Guidance Center
o. YMCA or YWCA
p. Other:
q. Don't know

9. Do you think social work is (a) for poor people only _____, or (b) for all sorts of people, including those who can pay for service_____?

10. Under what conditions would *you* seek help from a social worker?

11. When people are unemployed because there is no work for them, how do you think they should be supported?

12. Generally speaking, how do you think care should be provided for old people who have no close relatives and cannot support themselves?

13. If you had $15 to use for the following services, how would you divide it among them?
    a. Care of homeless children
    b. Care of needy aged
    c. Care of needy sick
    d. Relief to the unemployed
    e. Recreation for young people
    f. Hospitalization for tubercular patients
    g. Day-time care of children of working parents
    h. Help with difficulties of a personal nature
    i. Help to young people in choosing a job
    j. Citizenship training
    k. Unified planning of welfare work
    l. Rehabilitation of veterans
    m. Care of mentally ill
    n. Control of contagious diseases
    o. Prevention of cruelty to animals
    p. Care of alcoholics

14. How important do you think it is for an institution where children are cared for to have someone on duty who would study the personal problems of each child, keep in touch with his home, and assist him in making a good adjustment?
    Very Important_____ Important_____ Not so Important_____ Don't know_____

15. How important do you think it is to have a supervised place for young people to get together in your neighborhood?
    Very Important_____ Important_____ Not so Important_____ Don't know_____

16. Suppose a friend of yours were expecting a baby and asked you how she could get into a class on caring for

herself and the child. Where would you suggest she go to find out about such classes?

17. If you needed the services of a nurse in your home, how would you try to find one?

18. Would you mind telling me your idea of a social worker?

Name of interviewee_____ Address _____

Telephone (if none, be sure to indicate):_____

Age: 21–34_____ 35–49_____ 50 and over_____

Economic: A_____ B_____ C_____ D_____
          N_____

Education (years schooling completed):_____

Occupation of interviewee:

Professional	Salaried—executive	Retired
Proprietor	Wages—factory	Unemployed
Housekeeper	Wages—other	Student
Salaried—minor		

Occupation of head of family: _____

APPENDIX B

THE STORY OF ROSALIND

Many casework agencies believe that they must give thoughtful training to volunteers, to help them become useful to the agencies and to get satisfaction out of their work. The study of case material is a productive part of such training.

As we suggested in Chapter VI, the Jewish Family Service Association of Cleveland, in its Big Brother and Big Sister work, provides training for volunteers. The following case story—with a presentation first by the caseworker and then by the volunteer— proved so useful that we reproduce it here.

First we give the account of the caseworker, Lillian G. Greenberg:

I am going to tell you the story of Rosalind. The theme of this meeting, I was told, would be "A Tree Grows in Cleveland." I am sorry that my story does not parallel the story of the little girl in Brooklyn who had a tree to hide away in, to give her shelter and protection and encouragement. I would like to present Rosalind herself as a tree. Even as I say this, I recognize that my allegory is a little far fetched. A tree implies strength, stability. Rosalind is not like that. Shoots which should long have disappeared if our tree had had normal development, still persist. Because they do persist, our tree cannot grow straight. It is distorted, and at times ugly. We have a right to be concerned about it; an obligation to direct and strengthen it.

Before we can live up to our obligation, we must examine

the tree, see what it is really like, how it got this way. When we understand this, we can begin to think how we can help.

I first met Rosalind before I was her social worker. The playschool consulted me because she was making a poor adjustment there, was selfish, self-willed, sly, stubborn, demanding, unco-operative, obnoxious. A lot of adjectives to apply to a little girl not quite ten. The adjectives did not really describe Rosalind to me. I did not know what she was really like. I soon had an opportunity to see for myself. Rosalind was always asking for things. Demanding? She always insisted on doing things her own way. Self-willed? Stubborn? She was always there, underfoot, forcing herself upon the attention of the teachers. Sly? Selfish? Obnoxious? I still did not know. She acted as if she were all these things, but something did not quite ring true. She was always asking for things, but really did not seem to want them. Why did she keep on asking? The notice and attention she was getting from the teachers were frequently unpleasant. Why did she go after them? What was she accomplishing? What was behind it?

I was glad I was to be Rosalind's caseworker. I could now really get to know her. I would have to get behind the adjectives to Rosalind herself. I went back to the record.

The Jewish Family Service Association first met Rosalind the year she was born. Her father came for help because he and his wife were not getting along. Her mother had no use for her husband. She felt far superior to him and resented his insistence that they have a home of their own away from her parents. She preferred to live with her family. He could live with them too if he behaved himself; if not, well, he could go. As for Rosalind—the mother never wanted a child. Rosalind was an "accident," resented even before she was born. The mother felt she was still too young—only twenty, a child really—to be tied to an infant.

Rosalind's father was too weak, too helpless to cope with the situation. He gave in for the sake of peace.

It was tragic that our agency could not help ten years ago. The mother resented our "intrusion." As far as she was concerned, there was no problem, except Rosalind, and Rosalind would outgrow her meanness in time.

Rosalind did grow; somehow she grew. Uncared for, unwanted, unloved, she grew. Her mother told a social worker that Rosalind was a cranky baby. Always crying, never slept, just would not eat. She demanded a lot of attention.

This is the first year of her life; it sounds familiar.

I would like to stop here a moment and ask you to imagine with me what might have happened to Rosalind if she had been a good baby, never cried, was no problem. I wonder whether she would not have been one of those babies who "happen" to die in their infancy. If, somehow, she had managed to survive, I imagined her as a very crushed, frightened child, not even able to succeed as well as she has been doing as Rosalind. I think that we see in her "crankiness" an instinctual fight to survive. I use "crankiness" in quotation marks because this is not the word that we really mean, to describe her efforts to make her wants known, to make herself recognized. She *acts* cranky. Actually she is helpless and frightened and in need of the most elemental kind of care.

We see Rosalind a year later. Let me quote from our record of this period. "Rosalind is extremely thin, her legs and arms have practically no flesh on them. Her face is pale, her features sharply delineated. She has light, thin, stringy hair which falls untidily to her shoulders. Her mother stated unemotionally that she could not stand the sight of her." During that year her parents had separated and become reconciled several times. There were always fearful arguments, frequently developing into fights. There was no place of safety for Rosalind, for each parent tried to use her against the other.

At two years of age, Rosalind cries easily, she still soils herself. Her mother has made only half-hearted attempts to train her.

She is not doing well. She is just managing to hold on, little changed from a year ago. Usually a child makes great progress from the first to the second year of life.

Let us look at Rosalind at three. Again the same observations are made in the social record. In addition "Rosalind and her mother quarrel constantly, the mother reminding her from time to time how much she dislikes her." From a hospital record several months later, "Rosalind uses many tricks and devices to direct attention toward herself."

Throughout her life, Rosalind has been using devices to direct attention toward herself. This is essential. Without attention she could not survive as an infant. All babies cry in the first year of their lives to indicate that they are hungry or uncomfortable or ill. Rosalind had to cry harder, louder, to get her mother to hear her. She has had to fight harder to survive in the barren soil which her parents provided. It took all her energies to accomplish this.

I am about to state an important clue to the understanding of Rosalind: Rosalind's behavior is no different today from what it was when she was a little girl of two and three. She has not had the energy to develop into a ten-year-old little girl. Except that many things have happened to heighten and emphasize and reinforce the experience of her first three years, the description I have just read to you is the description of Rosalind when I first met her. We can understand Rosalind better when we think of her as a little girl of two or three. It is hard to understand a child of ten who acts like a child of three.

We must recognize that her behavior accomplished something for Rosalind: She made herself noticed by her parents. At least they knew she was there. If they could not love her, at least they cared enough to scold or strike her. To obtain even such results is a big job, a twenty-four-hour-a-day job; because if she were to let up, they would forget about her and she would lose them, and then she would be lost. She would not belong anywhere, would not have anything, would not be anybody. She had to have her parents' attention and she devised the tools to achieve this end.

When Rosalind started school, she had only these social tools to bring with her. She knew from long and bitter experience that adults did not like her, did not care about her, would ignore her if she let them. She did not let them. She had a terrible time in school, fighting, lying, cheating, demanding.

We wonder, "Could she learn that she does not have to be this way in school? That it would be better for her if she could act differently?" She could not learn. She is bright intellectually, true. But her emotions are those of a little two- or three-year-old child. These emotions have to be recognized and dealt with.

The school could not do this. I will let Dr. Luckey tell you why. The school had a serious problem on its hands. The school did all it could to help, but it is not equipped to deal with a child of three in a classroom of children, seven, eight, or nine. What Rosalind succeeded in learning at school, along with very little academic information, was that adults really did not understand her, really did not love her, really did want to get rid of her—and she must not let them.

About this time, many people became concerned about Rosalind and were anxious to help her. If the tree cannot grow because the soil is so poor, let us uproot it and plant it in richer soil. They reasoned: if Rosalind is what she is because her parents do not love her, let us place her where she will be loved and cared for.

About the time that Rosalind could no longer be tolerated in school and was to be expelled, she was placed at Bellefaire (a children's institution). This step was taken after careful thought. By this time she was much too disturbed to be able to become a member in a family group. She would need preparation, perhaps a less personal setting. Her mother was happy to get rid of her. Her father struggled with the idea a little but gave in, and Rosalind entered Bellefaire.

She did not get along. Mr. Rawley will tell you how much she did not get along. She could not be trusted, she was mean and stubborn and demanding. She acted like a little savage. A two-year-old child sometimes is a little savage. No one could love such a child, it seemed. She could not love anyone.

No one? This had to be tested.

Rosalind met her Big Sister about eighteen months ago. Mrs. Kushner will tell you about her contact with Rosalind and perhaps we can understand what happened better now in light of what we know. So far Mrs. Kushner has been the one person who has given kindness freely, unbidden. We would hope that Rosalind could now feel that such a miracle is possible, that someone could really love her, and relax a little—not fight so hard. We are not surprised, however, that this has not happened. It will take a great deal of living experience to teach Rosalind to unlearn what she has learned in ten years. We would have to presuppose certain conditions, if she can be protected from further hurt, and she must be offered a steady, uninterrupted nourishment of love and understanding before we can get under the barriers which she has set up to protect herself.

Unfortunately we cannot realize these conditions. We have little control over what happens to her. Rosalind is no longer at Bellefaire; she is back home. She is home because she chooses to be there, because she ran back, because she could not stay away.

By arranging for her to go to Bellefaire, we took a short cut in which she was not ready to join us. She had struggled for eight years to keep her parents aware of her. She fought not to let them forget her. Bellefaire represented a danger for her. By being out of her parents' sight, she was also being out of their minds and she could not take that. She had to return to the fight. She will be fighting. When she fights, sometimes she will not look pretty, she will look selfish, self-willed, sly, stubborn, demanding, unco-operative, obnoxious. But now we know her a little and we will not be deceived by the multitude of adjectives.

What can we do to help? We cannot do anything for Rosalind. We can only hope to be able to help her do something for herself. We cannot change her parents. They are too confused, too self-centered to be interested. We cannot take Rosalind away from her home; she will not go. Perhaps we cannot help her, perhaps the roots are so firmly implanted, so solidly established that we can do little. But perhaps, if we are as persistent in giving as she is in demanding, if we can pass every test she puts before us, we can teach her to trust us a little, and if we are faithful to the trust, perhaps, little by little we can help her to extend it to the world around her.

I have no optimistic hopes. We might see little progress after we have done the best we know how. If we do see a little progress, even if it is over a long period of time, we should be satisfied.

I think that we should feel justified in working very hard to strengthen our tree, not only for the tree itself, although that is a great deal, but also for the seeds which this tree will give forth and the effect which this tree will have on its seeds.

After Miss Greenberg had told this story, the volunteer, Mrs. Benjamin Kushner, gave the following account of her work with Rosalind:

When our conference, assigning me to Rosalind, was over I wondered whether I was really going to be able to help this child who needed so much love and affection. "Worried" is the word for the way I felt. I was glad, though, that I had arranged to return that afternoon to meet Rosalind, as I could not have stood the suspense of wondering what she was actually like, how she would take to me, or I to her.

Since Rosalind and her caseworker had discussed her having a Big Sister, she was not surprised when she was called to meet me [at Bellefaire]. As she came into her cottage living room, timidly, shyly, and slowly, I could not help being surprised, as it did not seem possible that this self-conscious, small, wistful child was capable of the behavior described to me earlier that day. In fact, throughout our friendship, for one year and eight months, very few of her disturbing and upsetting ways came up in relation to me or members of my family.

For the first few months, when we were just getting acquainted, I frankly was under considerable strain, as I never knew what to expect, and in a way expected the worst. I always felt, too, that Rosalind was not sure about me, as she told her caseworker the only reason she went with me was because "I needed her." Actually we did very simple things, which were suggested by the caseworker and our supervisor in our frequent conferences. Knowing how important regular and consistent contact was for Rosalind, we planned that Wednesdays would be the day we would spend together. I usually called for her at school, then we did some shopping on the way home, and on arriving home, made preparations for dinner, or baked, or did some household chore. Rosalind seemed to like all this. She gobbled up the snack of milk and cake I usually had for her, and to everyone's surprise, always ate heartily at dinner, in contrast to her refusal to eat and pickiness with food both at home and at Bellefaire.

By having her help me in whatever had to be done, I had an opportunity to praise her for little things she did well and to let her know that I thought she was all right.

When she said she liked mashed potatoes, I let her do the mashing. The hard-boiled eggs she had a preference for, she prepared and peeled. She was the one who took the cookies off the cookie sheet because she had helped mix the batter so well. She folded towels very neatly for me while I ironed. She drew pictures for us with crayons and won praise from the whole family.

She always has had complete freedom of the house. Though I left odd nickels and pennies once in obvious places, they were not so much as touched by Rosalind, though at Bellefaire and at school she had the habit of "borrowing," then forgetting to return what she took. She often spent considerable time in my daughter's room, combing her hair, and looking over the things on her dressing room table, but nothing was ever missing.

After a few months I began to relax with Rosalind. I no longer expected her to act up, as nothing had happened so far to make me think she would. My daughter and she became fast friends during this time. Rosalind could hardly wait for Louise to come home for dinner as she was "so hungry"—yet she waited. The two played ping-pong, played the piano, and sang songs, Rosalind also danced for us—enjoying the singing and dancing tremendously. My mother also became interested in Rosalind, who took "a shine" to her.

By the end of three months, in one of our conferences, I learned that Rosalind was showing considerable improvement in her school work. She was eating a little better at Bellefaire. She had from time to time complained about the breakfasts they had, but when I casually remarked that they seemed to be the same as most people had, this seemed to have some effect on her. I learned too that she anxiously waited for me on the days I was to call for her. When she was sick because of measles, she used to announce to everyone, on the day I was coming, "My Big Sister is coming today!" I knew we were coming closer.

239

There were other reasons to make me think this. Rosalind began doing things, I suppose, to test how I really felt about her. She had promised to bring all the cookies for their school party, and implied she expected me to make them for her. I talked over rationing with her, showing her why I could not do all that, and indicated she would have to get herself out of this promise. I got across to her that this was something she should have talked over with me earlier. She managed to get out of this successfully. Again, she began to make it obvious, by a variety of noises, that she would like some of the baked goods or candy we passed in the markets where we frequently shopped. I mentioned that we were going to have those the minute we got home, and gradually she became less obvious about it. Also, she stopped being helpful to the degree she was before, and frequently had to be reminded that she was the one who could set the table so well, and so competently helped clear it away.

When Rosalind's birthday came, and we had a birthday cake with candles, and a small gift from each one in the family, she was speechless with surprise and excitement. She had never been given such a celebration for herself before.

I had occasion to be out of town twice during that first summer of our friendship, and both times Rosalind, I learned, was upset by my going, fearing I would not return. She was delighted on my return, and the second time actually threw her arms around me and kissed me!

Toward the end of the summer, she began to talk about wanting to go home. She spoke more frequently of her parents, mentioning their promises to take her home for visits which never happened. She also began to talk about sleeping at my house. Just about this time, too, she actually forgot two or three dates which we had made. It was hard for us to know what was happening to her, but we all thought she needed some more permanent placement like a foster home to give her the security she needed to continue growing.

In our conferences in late fall and early spring, I learned that Rosalind's behavior at Bellefaire was becoming steadily worse. She was again wetting and soiling her bed regularly, and was again fussing over food and refusing to eat. She was refusing to do anything the cottage mother asked her to. She also began stealing again from the other children who, she said, did not like her, and stole from her. As you can imagine, I was quite surprised to learn how different her behavior was when she was not with me. . . .

By March, things apparently reached a climax inside Rosalind, and she ran away from Bellefaire—to her own home. I knew nothing of this until she suddenly appeared at my cooking class at the Council Educational Alliance one afternoon. She had told the registrar she "simply must be in Mrs. Kushner's class." She continued to come for the rest of the sessions, and co-operated well. I thought that with her return home, her mother would object to her friendship with me, but instead she has been pleasant, friendly, and willing for me to spend as much time as I cared with Rosalind. I noticed that Rosalind was being left alone a great deal, even when she was sick with chicken-pox. Her father works on the night shift and her mother seems never to be home. According to the caseworker, neither father nor mother wished Rosalind to come home, and the mother openly indicated that Rosalind tied her down, kept her from going out when she pleased and made demands on her. This is probably true, as Rosalind, when I have seen her, spends all her time trying to win her mother over. She caresses her, tries to kiss her, and tries to gain her attention constantly. Her mother, on the other hand, brushes her off, never gives her a smile, let alone approval.

This summer, Rosalind attended the Council Educational Alliance playschool, where I later did some volunteer work—I learned she was always in the office complaining about being mistreated and trying to get the attention of the teachers. We continued seeing each other almost every week, and again celebrated her birthday, as her mother did nothing about it, even though I offered to help. Recently she asked again, "When am I coming to sleep over at your house?" She implied that I was breaking a promise just like her mother who "always breaks promises."

I have tried, with the help given me, to do and say the things which would get across to Rosalind the fact that I liked her and would not let her down. I have also handled her just as I handled my own children, giving her small chores to do, making foods she would like but not catering to her too much, and praising her for any simple chore which she did. Having been forewarned that she might wish to hurt me by acting contrary, I tried, and think I succeeded fairly well, in showing no upset at her occasional refusal to eat certain foods, to her poor grades in school, or to her complaints about Bellefaire.

Now that she is home, her manners are getting worse, her stuttering has increased, and her eating habits are worse again. I am not sure just what I can mean to Rosalind, seeing her less frequently than I did, or how I can help her from this point on. She is trying to win her mother, and still is holding on to me. She has said to me, "I don't want you to have any other little friends at Bellefaire. You are my friend." She continually asks about sleeping at my house, yet I have hesitated because I have not been sure what it will mean to her.

These accounts of the Jewish Family Service Association's work with Rosalind have a double interest. First, of course, as a way of showing how an agency tried to help one troubled human being. And second, as a story which is not a success story, and for that reason provides challenging material for discussion.